CHARLES GAVAN DUFFY
Patriot and Statesman

CHARLES GAVAN DUFFY

Patriot and Statesman

The Story of Charles Gavan Duffy (1816-1903)

By

LEON Ó BROIN

DUBLIN
JAMES DUFFY & CO., LTD.
1967

PRINTED BY CAHILL AND CO. LTD., IN THE REPUBLIC
OF IRELAND, AT PARKGATE PRINTING WORKS, DUBLIN.

Contents

\

Acknowledgments

I AM happy and honoured to have been asked by James Duffy & Co. to write this book in order to mark the 150th anniversary of the birth of Charles Gavan Duffy. He, in a sense, can be said to have " made " the firm by engaging it to publish *The Ballad Poetry of Ireland*, *The Spirit of the Nation*, and other literary by-products of the Young Ireland movement. I am doubly pleased because it was also the wish of my friend, Louise Gavan Duffy, that I should write her father's " life ". In doing so, I had her help at every stage; she read the script more than once, supplied background information and personal details which were not otherwise obtainable as well as a copy of the Chronicle of the Hughes Family and very generously made me a present of her father's annotated scrapbook *Ars Vitae* which contains some illuminating passages of self-examination. The use I have made of this material will give my book, I hope, some value as a work of reference. Go gcúití Dia do chineáltas leat, a Lúise.

I should also like to thank Monica Starke of Melbourne, who is a great-granddaughter of Duffy, Bríd McGrath of the Irish State Paper Office, Eoin P. Ó Caoimh and Joan Lally for material assistance in the preparation of the book; and also the librarians and staffs of the National Library of Ireland, Trinity College, Dublin, the Royal Irish Academy, the Royal Dublin Society, the Dublin Corporation Libraries, and the Irish Folklore Institute for their unfailing helpfulness.

As regards the shape of the book, it will be apparent that I have closely followed the main lines of Duffy's autobiographical works but I have not hesitated to qualify his judgments on matters of major controversy where that appeared necessary.   A list of sources is given at the end of the book.

Dublin   LEON Ó BROIN.
August, 1966.

CHARLES GAVAN DUFFY was born in the town of Monaghan
on Good Friday the 12th April, 1816. His father, John
Duffy, was a shopkeeper who had accumulated considerable
property at a time when the Ulster Catholics were slowly
lifting their heads. His mother, Anne Gavan, was the
daughter of a gentleman farmer who had likewise succeeded
in emerging from " the trampled multitude ". Charles was
only ten years of age, and the youngest of six children, when
his father died but he already had a fair understanding of
Ireland's political condition for, as he said, " the oppressed
learn their wrongs early and I knew vaguely that Catholic
emancipation meant the deliverance of our race from the
subjection of Orange ascendancy in which we had habitually
lived ". He was passionately religious. When he was sent
to bed at nightfall he took a coarse board with him to kneel
upon under the blanket for fear his prayers might be " too
luxurious "; and for years he read controversial books so as
to be able to defend the mysteries of his faith.

He first went to a " poor school ", a successor of the hedge
schools of an earlier generation, where a one-handed man
strove to control a handful of barefooted and ragged boys,
but later, at the instance of his elder sister and with the consent of his guardian, a Parish Priest, he became the first
Catholic boy to enter the classical academy in the town that
was taught by a Presbyterian minister and where the pupils
were the well-to-do sons of Monaghan and the neighbouring

counties.　Here he was never allowed to forget that he belonged to the race who were beaten at the Boyne.

Charles benefited, however, from the standard teaching of the school and even more from the books he found in his guardian's library.　And while his connection with the academy ended abruptly he continued to study at home with the assistance of a young man preparing for Maynooth.　A new passion was coming into his life, one that was to last all his days, the determination to love and serve his country. This was fed by everything he saw and heard around him, by the local folklore in which he immersed himself, but especially by his talks with three friends who by a happy accident represented three totally distinct elements of Irish society.　One was Matt Trimble, son of a British army officer, who was afterwards an occasional writer in *The Nation*; another was Henry MacManus, the artist, who later, with John Hogan, the sculptor, presented a National Cap to O'Connell at the monster meeting of Mullaghmast ; the third was Terence Bellew MacManus, who later stood in arms in Ballingarry. Duffy and Terence Bellew MacManus spent their Sunday afternoons rambling through the countryside together, listening to the Orange drums and speculating what might be done to regain for their people the position that had been taken from them. The Orange processions made it impossible for them to forget the past and, as every Orange lodge had a liberal supply of arms, these were used freely and provocatively at the annual Twelfth of July celebration. Duffy saw a Catholic butcher shot in the street by a gun fired on one of these occasions; he had spoken offensively or perhaps thrown a shoe or stone, but, whatever his offence, death was the immediate penalty. He was carried to the grave in a coffin festooned with red ribbons to signify that he had been murdered, but no prosecution followed. Not long before this, the Peep o' Day Boys, in support of the Protestant landlords, had given Catholic farmers in

Armagh Cromwell's choice of " to Hell or Connaught " and
the story of what the dispossessed farmers suffered as a
result of this ultimatum inflamed young Duffy's mind.
Religious persecution was not a thing of the past : it was
actively present and called for redress. The question was,
how? A Quaker neighbour who had been a United Irishman
a generation earlier laughed at the idea that it was a question of kings and governments. What mattered was the land
from which the people got their bread. " In '98," he said,
" we spouted Gallic sentiments and sang the Marseillaise
and the Shan van Vogt . . . while what we ought to have
borrowed from France was their sagacious idea of bundling
the landlords out of doors and putting the tenants in their
shoes."

Duffy's three brothers died before he reached manhood.
His own health was feeble and uncertain and was a constant
preoccupation throughout what proved to be an abnormally
long life. From a health journal which came his way he
adopted a maxim which served him well : keep your head
cool, your feet dry, and your skin clean, your digestion
regular, and a fig for the doctor. He had begun to write—
chapters of a novel, first, and some scenes of a play—and
was probably thinking of taking up journalism, when one
day "a stately venerable gentleman" walked into his
mother's house and asked his help in promoting a newspaper,
The Northern Herald, he was about to start in Belfast. This
was the United Irishman, Charles Hamilton Teeling, who in
the previous generation had swept the British forces out of
two counties, and might have swept them out of two and
thirty but for adverse accidents. And Duffy reflected that
what men had done before they might do again—and do
better. This encounter set him off reading all the books he
could buy or borrow so that he gradually came to understand the epic of Irish resistance. He sent scraps of prose
and verse to Teeling for his paper, and the more he wrote

the more the desire grew in him to be a professional writer. He was not a precocious writer, however. He formed his style slowly. He never believed that writing was solely an inspiration; rather was it an art to be cultivated.

He made his first contacts with practical politics in the Monaghan Election in 1834, and by acting as secretary to a group of Catholics and Liberals, that included Teeling, who presented an address to the Lord Lieutenant as he toured the province of Ulster. This unique occasion was boycotted by the gentry, for Mulgrave was an unusual viceroy in that he received Protestants and Catholics on equal terms, treated prisoners, among them convicted rebels, with clemency, and was in consequence hailed by the Orange press as Tyrconnell O'Mulgrave. Duffy must have carried out his duties impressively, for Teeling urged him to pursue his education further by going to Trinity College, Dublin, the only existing university institution; but because of the anti-Catholic atmosphere of the college, Duffy's guardian refused to let him go.

Duffy, however, got to Dublin with his friend MacManus who was taking up a job as a shop assistant, and was himself accepted in 1836 as a trainee on the staff of *The Morning Register*, the Catholic Association's daily. His first surprise was to find that the editors of the three Catholic papers that supported O'Connell were all Protestants while the outstanding Protestant organ had Catholics as its co-editors. The reporters were a blasé lot, in whom national spirit had evaporated with the collapse of the first Repeal movement. A greater surprise and disappointment was O'Connell himself whom he began to see daily in the Courts and at public meetings in Conciliation Hall and elsewhere. He was not the romantic figure he had conceived, the successor of Owen Roe, Sarsfield and Grattan, but a practical man of affairs, in whom humour, fierceness, vulgarity and a capacity for cold logical analysis were mixed. Duffy fell foul of

O'Connell when the Liberator alleged that a speech attributed to him in *The Register* was a misrepresentation. *The Register* insisted on the accuracy of the report and this drove O'Connell to attack the paper and reporters in general at a meeting of the Precursor Society. Duffy, who was present, immediately gathered up his papers and walked out followed by three colleagues. The demonstration led to a reconciliation with *The Register*, and O'Connell ceased abusing reporters.

Duffy was keen on asserting the rights of newspapermen and actually proposed the formation of the press association that came into being in May, 1838, but was short-lived. To that association, again on Duffy's motion, members of the staffs of periodicals were admitted, including James Clarence Mangan, whom he introduced as one of the most accomplished and popular writers for the *University Magazine*.

Duffy went through the gamut of journalism on no more than £1 a week. He lived modestly and saved money to buy books, while relying on a circulating library to get the novels of Griffin and Banim, and *Blackwood's* and the *Edinburgh Review* which were then in their ripe middle age. In April, 1839, he became the first editor of a Belfast bi-weekly, *The Vindicator*, which had been established by some of the Catholics in that city in support of the national leader : and in August of the same year he bought it out. He " gave the paper a tone of originality and movement which no other paper then existing had. . . . He wrote in favour of radicalism and home manufactures, projected reading clubs, revived local traditions, composed verses and got others to write them also ". And he had his reward in a sale of 1,300 copies which was remarkable in that time and in the heart of the enemy's quarters. The Catholics of the North were rarely consulted on political matters, and were ordinarily expected to follow the lead of the Whigs, who at the same time denied them a fair share of the municipal

offices.   Duffy encouraged them to speak out for themselves,
to be prepared to drop the Whigs and to work under leaders
of their own choosing, if that should become necessary.   His
urging had immediate results: Repeal meetings were organised all over the Northern counties to the delight of O'Connell
and to the fury of the Orange press.   O'Connell declared
that the spirit of the North had been aroused; " that excellent
journal, *The Vindicator*, had caused a new light to dawn
upon the people of Ulster, and still continues to do incal-
culable service to the cause of freedom ".   Ninety-three
meetings were held in one day, and O'Connell then
announced to the stupefaction of many that he would hold a
provincial meeting in Belfast itself!   The Tory papers defied
him to come to the Orange capital but O'Connell made his
way into the city, eluding the Orangemen who gathered at
various points along the route to deny him entry.   Such was
the atmosphere, however, with a mob in command who
broke every pane of glass in *The Vindicator* office that a
public meeting was out of the question.   O'Connell, however,
spoke to fifteen hundred people indoors, and Duffy helped
to smuggle him out of the city on his return journey.   This
was in January, 1841.

Duffy while in Belfast did two other things of importance.
He followed a course in philosophy at the Royal Academical
Institution, and he wooed and won the hand of Emily
MacLaughlin, the daughter of a well-to-do Catholic mer-
chant.   He had ambition, but his talents requiring a wider
scope for their exercise he turned to Dublin with the dual
object of starting a paper there and of going to the Bar, a
profession that was linked with the political career that had
opened before him.   He had enrolled as a student at King's
Inns in the Michaelmas Term, 1839, and three years later he
left Belfast and *The Vindicator* and settled in the capital
where, somewhat earlier, a young barrister, John Blake
Dillon, whom he had first met at the office of *The Morning*

Register, introduced him to Thomas Davis in the committee
room of the Repeal Association in the old Corn Exchange.
Dillon he found frank, manly, serious-minded, sympathetic
and confident; he had admired Duffy's own writing in *The
Vindicator* and had drawn Davis's attention to it.   Davis
pleased Duffy less: of his ability and sincerity he had no
doubt—he knew of his contributions to *The Citizen,* lately
become *The Dublin Monthly Magazine*—but he appeared to
be dogmatic and self-opinionated. However, both these men
were fundamentally unlike any of those he had met in
journalism and he opened up to them the project of a new
national newspaper, which would contain most of the char-
acteristic features of *The Vindicator.*   This was excellent
news for them, for as Davis put it, they had long wanted to
see a paper that would be " more decided than Mr.
O'Connell's organs and less Romanist than *The Freeman's
Journal* ". The result was a conference under an elm tree
in the Phoenix Park facing Kilmainham and a decision to
establish a weekly with Duffy as its editor and proprietor.
The decision was a bold one in view of the fact that " Mr.
O'Connell's organs ", *The Freeman's Journal* and *The
Register,* were so solidly established, and a very risky one
for Duffy who was putting his limited fortune at stake. The
three men showed that they were under continental influence
by the decision to call the paper *The Nation* after the Paris
journal of that name and by defining in their prospectus the
nationality which was their first great object—as one which
would not only raise the Irish people from their poverty
by securing them the blessings of a domestic legislature but
would (as Mazzini was suggesting in his writings) influence
and purify them with a lofty and heroic love of country
and embrace Protestant, Catholic and dissenter, Milesian
and Cromwellian. The three men had their own particular
predilections as to what, inside those general lines, the paper
should emphasise. Duffy argued that what Ireland most

needed was education; without it nothing could be accomplished. Davis agreed, but added that they should make a special appeal for the help of the classes already educated, particularly the Protestant middle class. Duffy did not oppose this, but doubted whether the Protestants of Ulster would co-operate at all, for, in his view, Tone and Russell and the other men of 1798 had no successors. As for Dillon, his primary concern was with the condition of the peasantry in Connacht so that it was important to take up the land question.

Duffy discovered after some time that his first impressions of Davis were " extremely unjust ". They became the closest of friends, and could discuss intimate matters, even their attitudes to women. Davis confessed that his memory could not go back to the time he was not in love. We do not know whether this drew any admission from Duffy but he left among his papers a note which described his feelings towards the other sex at various ages. " At eight years," he wrote, " I felt a passionate attachment for a child of my own age. At eleven or twelve my mind was agitated with vague dreams and fantasies of a mistress won by wonderful personal achievements. At fifteen I loved a girl who was my elder and better. I thought her a goddess, she thought me a fool. And faith she was most in the right. At seventeen first awoke a new sensation turbulent and fierce and meaning I knew not what. At one and twenty I was unstained by any breach of the sixth commandment."

2

The Nation's first number appeared on the 15th October, 1842. It had a spectacular success. Within a few weeks the paper, which combined news, literary criticism, poetry and social and political commentary, was being read all over the country; those who could not afford sixpence to buy it, borrowed it or perused it in the Repeal Reading Rooms. Within three years it had acquired fame outside Ireland and brought a measure of affluence to Duffy. Its chief claim, he thought, was the frankness with which it discussed the truths which had formerly been only heard in whispers. The case of Ireland was no longer the lament of a beggar who showed his sores to excite passion, but the remonstrance of an injured and angry partner, who insisted either on fair play or an end to the partnership. The excesses of the landlords were boldly exposed, and the principles of public polity applied to the operations of the Government, but it had other qualities besides, those which Lecky noted when he said that seldom had a journal exhibited a more splendid combination of eloquence, poetry and reasoning than did *The Nation* under Gavan Duffy's editorship. He insisted that the first want of the Irish people was the knowledge long withheld by a jealous master. From ignorance came sycophancy. Slaves looked upon their masters with superstitious awe; upon themselves with superstitious distrust. Therefore, he repeated, educate that you may be free. He was thinking of a comprehensive reforming freedom, one that concerned the individual Irishman as well as the Irish nation. "The slave's vice of paltering with the truth," he wrote, "clings to our people like the rust of their chains."

The poetry side of the paper was particularly effective.

Duffy in *The Vindicator* had begun the experiment of appealing to the people in passionate popular verse, a collection of which later appeared in book form as *The Ballad Poetry of Ireland*. He did not know any Irish but he realised that the translations of the songs he had heard in his youth were an element that linked the Irish people with their past and that could be used to animate their political ambitions. He had also tried his hand at writing original ballad poetry and had encouraged some of his friends, among them James Clarence Mangan, a real poet with no interest in politics, to do the same. He repeated this experiment in *The Nation*, beginning with the publication of his own *Fág a' Bealach* in the third issue.

" Hope no more for Fatherland ;
        All its ranks are thinned or broken,"
Long a base and coward band
        Recreant words like these have spoken.
        But *we* preach a land awoken—
Fatherland is true and tried,
        As your fears are false and hollow,
Slaves and dastards, stand aside!
        Knaves and traitors, fág a' bealach!

Know, ye suffering brethren ours,
        Might is strong, but Right is stronger!
Saxon wiles or Saxon pow'rs
        Can enslave our land no longer
        Than your own dissensions wrong her.
Be ye one in might and mind ;
        Quit the mire where cravens wallow ;
And your foes shall flee like wind
        From your fearless fág a' bealach!

Thus the mighty multitude
    Speak in accents hoarse with sorrow;
We are fallen, but unsubdued;
    Show us whence we hope may borrow,
    And we'll fight your fight tomorrow.
Be but wise and true and brave,
    Where you lead us we will follow;
Hill and valley, rock and wave
    Soon shall hear our fág a' bealach!

Fling our banner to the wind,
    Studded o'er with names of glory;
Worth and wit, and might and mind,
    Poet young and patriot hoary
    Long shall make it shine in story.
Close your ranks! The moment's come—
    Now, ye men of Ireland, follow!
Friends of Freedom, charge them home!
    Foes of Freedom, fág a' bealach!

Of Duffy's historical ballads Lecky said that they had a fire and a strength which no similar compositions in Ireland had shown. His "Muster of the North", in which the Rising of 1641 was extolled, became the subject of a *Times* editorial in which literary merits were praised and meaning misrepresented with equal exaggeration. Or so Duffy said; but all the Tory journals in the empire saw it in the same light as the *Times*. The "Muster" became in fact the best-abused ballad in existence and one paper went so far as to say that the man who wrote it had the intellect and heart of Satan.

Davis followed Duffy's lead and was delighted to find that he could compose with facility; and gradually the idea spread until the whole corps of writers associated with the paper were writing in verse. A great deal of this was understandably of inferior quality but many rousing poems were written that have retained their popularity down to the present day, among them John Kells Ingram's "Memory of the Dead", which Lecky thought would hold a permanent place in English poetry, Davis's "The West's Asleep" and Michael Joseph Barry's "Step Together". Who has not heard the opening lines of John O'Hagan's "The Union"?

> How did they pass the Union?
>   By perjury and fraud;
> By slaves who sold their land for gold
>   As Judas sold his God;
> By all the savage acts that yet
>   Have followed England's track—
> The pitchcap and the bayonet,
>   The gibbet and the rack.
> And thus was passed the Union,
>   By Pitt and Castlereagh;
> Could Satan send for such an end
>   More worthy tools than they?

These, and many others, subsequently appeared in *The Spirit of the Nation*, a little book that ran into scores of editions and is still in print.

In view of *The Nation's* emphasis on balladry it was not surprising that Mrs. Thomas Carlyle remembered Duffy as " a writer of national songs " when he first came to London " to eat terms " with a view to being called to the English Bar. He had " the coarsest of human faces ", she thought, " decidedly as like a horse's as a man's ", which was neither complimentary nor borne out by Beatrice Franklin's well-known portrait, but she also found in him " one of the people I should get to think beautiful, there is so much of the power both of intellect and passion in his physiognomy." Other English women were more flattering. The Duffy they saw was " picturesque and effervescent ", " a delicious Irish-man ", in fact.

The unique character of *The Nation* owed a great deal to the intimate companionship that Duffy helped to foster among the contributors who could come to his office as often as they liked so that it became in fact the movement's headquarters. Saturday night was planning night : the inner group of five—Duffy, Davis, Dillon, Pigot and John O'Hagan —with some others met by arrangement in one another's houses and from tea-time to supper-time and on into the early hours literary and political projects were debated and decisions reached as to what was to be written and by whom. These meetings were kept secret for fear of suggesting " erroneous notions ". In this fashion high standards were achieved, the writers exposing themselves at these meetings, and in correspondence with each other, to frank criticism. Davis, from the start, was the chief leader writer and helped with the editing so as to enable Duffy to devote more time to the managerial side of the paper at which he was so good.

Most of *The Nation's* contributors discovered their literary talents in the politics of the paper but remained amateurs ; there were others, like Mangan and Carleton, whose interest in the paper was entirely professional. These never ceased to find in Duffy an editor who understood and appreciated them as few editors did. Mangan, a strange wraith-like figure, used steal into *The Nation* office once a week for a chat, but if any of Duffy's friends appeared whose " frothy speeches " he disliked he took flight on the instant. From about 1836 when Duffy first met him in Dublin he was on the closest terms with the poet and visited with him the family of Margaret Stackpoole for whom Mangan had a love that was not returned. The visits ended when Mangan began to suspect that Duffy was becoming interested in the young lady who was " a model of all that was witching and winning in women ". As time moved on

and Mangan became a slave to drugs or drink Duffy tried
desperately but unavailingly to save him from self-destruc-
tion. He paid him in advance for copy that was sometimes
not supplied and largely financed the publication of his
Anthologica Germanica. He also managed somehow to main-
tain a friendship with the lithe six-foot tall Carleton who
was much hated for abandoning the Catholic faith. Duffy
took no part in the campaign against him. On the contrary
he recognised Carleton's unique worth as a man who had
risen up from a humble cottage to describe a whole people
and persevered with him despite the depressing whine he
kept up about his desperate need of money. " If, my dear
Charles," Carleton once wrote, " you ever utter an impre-
cation against your worst enemy—have mercy—have mercy
—and do not let the bitter malediction be that God should
make him a Man of Genius in Ireland." Charles J. Kickham,
the Fenian author, noted how his friend Duffy kept a watchful eye on Ireland's unlucky children of genius, instancing
the case of Edward Walsh, the indigent poet-schoolmaster,
whom Duffy helped with respectable employment and whose
widow he later saved from the poorhouse.

The militant tone of the poetry of *The Nation* and the
constant looking backward was bound to be misunderstood,
both in Ireland and across the Channel. Samuel Ferguson
made the comment that " some of these fellows longed to
stick their skeins in the bowels of the Saxon " and the
friendly English literary critic, Leigh Hunt, wished that *The
Nation* would retain all its fire and generosity with none of
the *vi et armis* part of its spirit. He wanted the horrible
possibility of an appeal to arms in Ireland kept out of sight.
Like Lord Chancellor Plunket he recognised that the tone of
The Nation was Wolfe Tone. The Government were of the
same mind. The police were set to watch the young men
and their contacts, and Duffy discovered that a police agent,
a brother of the important historical writer, John Cornelius

O'Callaghan, who had contributed three items to the first issue of *The Nation*, was following him around. A search for papers was a possibility and writers for *The Nation* were warned to put their correspondence out of the way. "Any rash phrases," Davis told R. R. Madden, "could be used to persuade the Parliament that there was some plot here. There is not; we are too wise to conspire." Madden, who was living in England at the time, gathered from the newspapers that the agitation in Ireland might end in bloodshed, but Davis set his mind at rest. "You in England quite overrate the likelihood of war here. Unless the Government begin the contest either with their own troops or with an Orange mob, there will be no fight for the present. We are making more way with the upper classes than you fancy." Those people would not, yet at least, join the Repeal Association, but many of them were attracted by the Federal idea that had been sponsored by the Northern reformer, William Sharman Crawford, as an alternative to outright Repeal of the Union. Under Federalism Ireland would have a domestic legislature of a subordinate character rather along the lines of the Home Rule of later years. If the Federalist Party that was about to be formed, Davis continued, were managed by bold, clear-minded men, it would impose its own terms on England in two years. "We Repealers," he added, "hold peace and war in our hands. O'Connell could in three months have possession of Ireland, but he is adverse, wisely humanly adverse to fighting save in the last extremity. He prevailed in '29 by the *power* of fighting, not the *practice* of it; may he not do so again? You will say, no, for England is dead against us. What's the proof of her being so? I see little. On the contrary, I believe a portion of the intelligence and half the populace of England will aid us, if things go on peaceably, as they are going."

While armed rebellion was not then contemplated the glorification of national heroes and the stress on English

iniquity undoubtedly stimulated the feelings that produce
rebellion. And later on some of the Young Irelanders began
to express themselves in favour of a resort to physical force
instead of the moral suasion on which the Repeal movement
had hitherto relied. Thus Davis could write:

> The tribune's tongue or poet's pen
> May sow the seed in prostrate men,
> But 'tis the soldier's sword alone
> Can reap the harvest when 'tis grown.

To O'Connell, on the other hand, the use of force was un-
thinkable save in self-defence. He had no objection to com-
memorating the heroes of the remote past and he was at one
with *The Nation* group in desiring a union of all Irishmen
whatever their class or creed, but he differed from Davis,
for instance, in his attitude to the United Irishmen and particularly to Wolfe Tone whom he blamed for providing the
excuse for the Union. While Davis therefore could rhap-
sodise about the green grave at Bodenstown, O'Connell
regarded its occupant as a miscreant.

O'Connell had welcomed the accession of strength that *The
Nation* brought him. Though nearly seventy years of age
he was as vigorous and as brilliant as ever, the unquestioned
leader of the people, and a world figure whose every move
and word was widely reported. He had brought Ireland
out of obscurity, had lifted his people from the gutter and
made a democracy of them, had secured the emancipation
of Catholics throughout the British Empire, and had espoused
other movements of radical reform including the cause of
anti-slavery. Realist and pragmatist to his fingertips, he had
allowed the movement for the repeal of the Act of Union
to hang fire between 1835 and 1840 recognising that his
Whig allies were not prepared for any such measure; but in
1840, the emergence of a Tory government under his old

enemy, Sir Robert Peel, inspired him to renew the agitation. The Repeal Association was re-formed and the Repeal rent increased considerably. By the time *The Nation* came on the scene the agitation was already well under way. Within a further year a great transformation had occurred. A new soul, it was said, had come into Ireland as a result of this new paper which, while fully supporting O'Connell, introduced a more intense and emotional content into Irish nationalism.

The Government reacted by declaring that there was no power available to them " that would not be employed to resist Repeal, even if it meant civil war " and they flooded the country with soldiers to show that they were in deadly earnest. O'Connell had never the intention nor the means of resorting to force, but his speeches at this time gave the impression that the people would resist further provocation. He would violate no law and assail no enemy, he declared at Mallow, but there were others who would. Were Irishmen to be trampled under foot? he asked. They might trample on him, but it would be his dead body they would trample on, not the living man. Many people, therefore, were dismayed when, on the Government proclaiming a monster meeting called for Clontarf, O'Connell acquiesced in the face of a concentration of horse, foot and artillery. That decision, as Duffy put it, deprived the Repeal movement in a moment of half its dignity and all its terror; but on reflexion the Young Irelanders realised that the alternative to proceeding with the meeting and risking a mass slaughter was out of the question. So they swallowed their chagrin and turned their energies to projects of education and discipline.

Duffy now had his first experience of being arrested and of being charged, along with O'Connell and six other Repealers—two of them journalists like himself—with conspiring to excite ill-will among her Majesty's subjects, to weaken their confidence in the administration of justice, and

to obtain by unlawful methods a change in the constitution
and government of the country. They were tried in January-
February, 1844, by four Protestant judges, one of them a
notorious political partisan, and a jury on which no Catholic
was permitted to serve. The outcome was a term of
imprisonment which Duffy found, " as little unpleasant as a
holiday in a country-house ". The prisoners were allowed
to live together. They had two large gardens in which to
exercise, a sitting room and bedroom each, were allowed
visits from their friends and even to receive deputations.
They gave dinner parties, produced plays, and bishops vied
with each other for the favour of celebrating daily Mass
for them. Duffy continued to edit *The Nation* without inter-
ruption, and indeed arranged that it was printed with green
ink, the first week of their incarceration, to express hope
and confidence, and that the articles and verses that had
been pronounced seditious should be republished. An
important effect of the prosecution was to make William
Smith O'Brien the deputy leader of the Repeal movement.
He who had formerly led the Irish Liberals in the House
of Commons joined the Repeal Association after the collapse of the Clontarf meeting and in protest against the
coercion policy of the Tories. He was a man of very considerable ability and experience and has been well described
as perhaps the most upright as well as the least fortunate
of all Irish political leaders. At the end of three months
the prisoners were discharged on an appeal to the Judicial
Committee of the House of Lords and O'Connell was given
a delirious reception from the people organised by O'Brien
and Davis. Duffy was likewise fêted as he journeyed with
friends from Dublin to take up an invitation he had from
O'Connell to visit him at Derrynane. This was intended to be
a leisurely restful tour but the people wanted to honour the
State prisoner, and so they met him everywhere he went with
bands, bonfires, arches and addresses of greeting. In spite

of all the fuss Duffy enjoyed himself; the scenery was new to him and his mind was wide open to the historic associa-tions of the places he passed through, Kilkenny, New Ross, Waterford, Cork, Gougane Barra and Killarney. They made a detour through Cappoquin where they saw a vigorous young priest addressing the people in Irish by the light of a bonfire, and at Mount Melleray the newly arrived com-munity of Trappists transforming the barren fields. In Cork they visited a good friend, Father Theobald Mathew, whose temperance apostolate was reforming the character of the people. At Derrynane, by the Atlantic, O'Connell wel-comed them graciously and made them feel at home. The entertainment was on a princely scale: for breakfast alone there was " a pot roast or two, grilled fowl, smoking pota-toes, slim-cake, delicious fresh honey, home-made bread and baker's ditto, and added to these all the ordinary edibles and drinkables of a metropolitan table." There were letters awaiting Duffy from Davis, who was looking after the paper in his absence. " I am proud," he wrote in one, " of my dear, dear Munster having pleased you so much. I love it almost to tears at the thought." And in another, he begged Duffy to impress on O'Connell the need for more Repeal reading rooms and books. " Damn the ignorance of the people," he wrote, " but for that we should be lords of our own future; without that, much is insecure." Duffy had reported the results of his visits to schools, reading rooms, teetotal societies and bookshops. In some places there were no reading rooms; in others reading rooms with bookless shelves; and the books on view were " detestably English: no Irish novels, poems or plays except by accident ".

It seemed to some people that the way was open for a fresh advance; but O'Connell read the signs differently. Dur-ing his imprisonment he had become afraid of an unprepared popular rebellion and on his release he had hastened to issue a reminder that the greatest and most desirable of political changes could be achieved by moral means alone, and that no human revolution was worth the spilling of a single drop of human blood. It was, no doubt, he said on another occasion, a very fine thing to die for one's country, but in his opinion, one live patriot was worth a whole church-yard full of dead ones. The path of freedom would be long and arduous. This, Young Irelanders as they were now being called, were prepared to believe, but O'Connell astonished them by proposing to dissolve the Repeal Association and to replace it by another body free from the vulnerable features that the State had attributed to it in the course of the prosecution. This seemed to justify an Orange journal's remark that O'Connell had brought two feather beds to jail —one for himself, and the other for repeal. He did not press this proposal in the teeth of the opposition it aroused, but he again alarmed the young men when he expressed a preference for a Federal system " as tending more to the utility of Ireland and the maintenance of a connexion with England than the proposal of simple repeal". Duffy challenged this apparent change of policy in an open letter to O'Connell which he published in *The Nation* and which was immediately reprinted in scores of other papers, thereby giving particular solace to the English Tories who saw evidence in it of a division among O'Connell's followers. This publicity was galling to O'Connell. It stiffened him against the Young Irelanders who had been adopting an ascetical attitude to him that he understandably found irksome. They had been critical of him for surrounding himself with yes-men, for refusing to give an account of how the Repeal rent was expended and for helping his relatives and friends into Government jobs. His platform antics disgusted some of them also, while others thought that he had turned the Repeal Association into an almost wholly Catholic body.

An ultimate break with O'Connell was, therefore, a real possibility and Duffy's open letter did nothing to prevent it.

He wrote it in haste and without consulting his colleagues who were out of town. Davis was actually negotiating with the Federalists at the time. He was prepared to give Federalism a fair chance, while recognising that it could not be a final settlement, and he was sorry when O'Connell issued what was described as a recantation, for this taking up and dropping of Federalism could only do harm to a movement to which they were sympathetic. It could not do any good to O'Connell himself either; and Duffy was given the credit for having put the Liberator back on the lines. "How grateful I felt to heaven," wrote R. D. Williams, "that *The Nation* at least will be no party to a step that after all that has been said and sung and acted, must cover us with the laughter and contempt of Europe. Repeal is a magic word and it is trebly hazardous to resign even a sound that has become so holy to the heart of Ireland." And at a meeting in Limerick mention of Duffy's name evoked a great cheer.

More serious trouble with O'Connell occurred when Peel in 1845 proposed to increase the grant for Maynooth College and to establish colleges in Belfast, Cork and Galway to be affiliated to a Queen's University. The first of these proposals was unobjectionable, but the second which was designed to give the Catholic middle classes the educational advantages that had formerly only been open to Protestants and the better-off Catholics sparked off a conflict as to whether Catholic and Protestant students should be educated together or not. The Young Irelanders believed they should in order that prejudice and bigotry might be killed in the bud but the Young Liberator, as O'Connell's son John was called—it being recognised that he was being groomed for the succession—declared that an attempt was being made to undermine religion and morality in Ireland, and following his lead, O'Connell denounced the measure as a huge scheme of godless education. He wanted Catholic colleges to be sited in Cork and Galway,

Belfast college could be Presbyterian, while the existing
Trinity College, Dublin, could be left with the Protestants.
Davis advocated the English radical view that all the
colleges should be strictly undenominational, while Duffy
appeared to take a fairly common line that the colleges,
even if not Catholic in character, could be freed of anti-
Catholic objections. He saw education as the essential
and indispensable preliminary of freedom and was anxious
that the opportunity the Bill provided should not be missed.
He surmised that O'Connell's motive for rejecting the Bill
was to help the Whigs by preventing Peel from securing
any popular kudos. He could understand however that
O'Connell might be genuinely afraid of the measure en-
dangering the faith of Catholic students, but a Prime
Minister who desired to make peace with Ireland would
surely not oppose the enactment of the necessary safe-
guards.

While the bishops, who were primarily concerned, pon-
dered their attitude to the question, a great debate ensued
within the Repeal Association. Davis, in a long correspondence with O'Connell, discussed what he believed was
the threat of religious bigotry. O'Connell was no bigot,
however; he desired religious freedom all round and was
genuinely prepared to jettison Repeal if it prevented any
one Protestant or Catholic from believing or saying whatever he felt was consistent with truth. But he failed to
convince Davis of this.

The bishops duly announced their position. They were
willing to co-operate with the Government in founding provincial colleges but they pointed out the lack of provision
for the religious and moral discipline of the students and
other dangers to their faith and morals. They suggested
amendments which would make the measure acceptable.
At the next Association meeting O'Connell in a two hours'
speech interpreted the bishops' declaration as a rejection of

the scheme. He was supported in a wild speech by Michael George Conway, a young fellow who was taking revenge against the Young Irelanders for a slight he believed he had suffered at their hands. O'Connell, according to Duffy, cheered every offensive sentence in this speech and finally took off his cap and waved it over his head triumphantly. Later, when Davis was replying, O'Connell believing that Davis was suffering from Protestant monomania, constantly interrupted him and accused him of sneering at the Catholics.

He then made a second speech which ended with a peroration that has become famous. " The principle of the Bill has been supported," he said, " by Mr. Davis, and was advocated in a newspaper (*The Nation*) professing to be the organ of the Roman Catholic people of this country, but which I emphatically pronounce to be no such thing. The sections of politicians styling themselves The Young Ireland Party, anxious to rule the destinies of this country, start up and support this measure. There is no such party as that styled Young Ireland. There may be a few individuals who take that denomination on themselves. I am for Old Ireland. 'Tis time that this delusion should be put an end to. ' Young Ireland ' may play what pranks they please. But I do not envy them the name they rejoice in. I shall stand by Old Ireland ; and I have some slight notion that Old Ireland will stand by me."

Smith O'Brien and Henry Grattan the Younger protested, and the fundamentally generous O'Connell rose to withdraw the nickname of Young Ireland, as he understood its implied association of Davis and company with a reactionary English Tory group was resented. Davis, in a spirit of reconciliation, rejoined that he was glad to get rid of the assumption that there were factions in the Association. He and his friends, he said, were bound by a strong affection towards O'Connell; and as he spoke these words he broke into tears. The altercation thus ended on a happier note but blows had been

struck from which the Association never recovered. Distrust
and suspicion widened the breach. John O'Connell was
credited with circulating the story that Davis was a dangerous intriguing infidel and that his friends acquiesced in
his dark desires. This rumour made a serious impression on
the Catholic clergy and the sale of *The Nation* suffered in
consequence. Dillon could only find one priest in the whole
of the County Mayo who was not unfriendly to the paper.

While the Repeal Association began to show the effects of
this rift in a growing paralysis Davis renewed the attempt
to organise the Federalists. He first planned a quarterly
review and then proposed to buy over a Whig evening
paper that appeared three times a week and expressed
Federalist opinions. And Duffy was actually advising on
the doubtful economics of these ideas when he was summoned urgently one September morning in 1845 to Davis's
house in Baggot St. where to his horror he was shown the
lifeless corpse of the man he loved beyond any on earth.
Davis had died of scarlatina after only a week's illness. It
was, said Duffy, as if the light had suddenly gone out of
the sky. He likened the loss of Davis to the removal of
Ireland's guiding mind when Brian Boru died at Clontarf,
when Hugh O'Neill's life ended in exile, when Roger
O'Moore expired on the threshold of a great conflict and
when Owen Roe died leading the army which had conquered at Benburb. There was a large element of romantic
exaggeration in these comparisons for, in truth, Davis was
little known outside Dublin, so that if national calamity
had befallen them, the bulk of the Irish people were un-
aware of it. Duffy himself was better known, because he
had basked in the reflected glory of O'Connell during the
days they had spent together in Richmond Gaol. Davis
was, however, a potential figure of national dimensions and
many years afterwards he did become such a figure as the

result, principally, of the presentation of him in Duffy's widely read writings, and in occasional lines like these :

Oh! could you live as Davis lived—kind Heaven be his bed!—
With an eye to guide, and a hand to rule, and a calm and kingly head,
And a heart from whence, like a holy well, the soul of his land was fed—

Davis and Duffy had come to be regarded as Young Ireland's Siamese twins : their close associates rarely spoke or wrote about one of them without mentioning the other. Duffy conceded leadership in political thinking to Davis who was his senior by a year or two, but in business and organisational acumen, Duffy's contribution to the combination was of a higher order.

It never crossed his mind to dispute Davis's primacy in the evolution of the Young Ireland brand of nationalism in which were fused the Catholic democratic tradition and that of continental liberal radicalism associated in Ireland with the name of Wolfe Tone. He was himself a product of the former tradition and at the time he met Davis his vision was limited by the desire to set up again the Celtic race and the Catholic Church. " Davis it was who induced me," he said, " to aim ever after to bring all Irishmen of whatever stock into the confederacy to make Ireland a Nation." It was therefore a shock to him to discover after Davis's death that the man he idolised had taken umbrage just because some English journalists regarded Duffy as the original teacher of the " nationality " which *The Nation* disseminated. In a note found among his papers Davis insisted that the nationality theme had originated with him, and he wrote rather patronisingly about Duffy who, he said, had been editing " an ultra-Roman Catholic paper and was full of patriotism and ambition when he came to Dublin but had no distinct notion of national independence or national policy. That notion, he emphasised, belonged mainly to Trinity College Protestants, whereas Duffy's education and opinions were those of a Catholic English Radical and Benthamite education was his chief wish. However, Duffy's flexible mind soon caught up our purposes," Davis added, " and carried them into his writings with great clearness, zeal and genius ".

Duffy's flexible mind also enabled him to do other things. He finished his law studies, for instance, and was called to the Irish Bar within a month of Davis's death. " The practice at that time," he said, " was to impose an additional oath and an additional fee on Catholic barristers; the oath being some obsolete absurdity about the Pretender. I took the oath but refused to pay the fee (only half a crown), regarding it as a remnant of the penal laws, and left the Court to its remedy. I heard no more on the subject. . . ."

3

A few weeks later Duffy had to endure an even more personal grief than the death of Davis when his wife died of a slow consumption following the birth of their second child, John, who in his mature years became a Cabinet Minister in Australia. The first child, a girl whom Duffy called Anna Eva after his mother and the mother of all men, had not survived. Duffy was the recipient of a great volume of sympathy, and of promises to share the heavy burden of *The Nation* with him, but the men after Davis on whom he would have leaned most were no longer available to him. Dillon was under doctor's orders to winter in a warmer clime, O'Hagan and Pigot had gone to London to study for the English Bar, while McNevin, unknown to himself, was in an advanced stage of a fatal illness. There were men like McCarthy, Barry, Doheny and O'Neill-Daunt who gave Duffy an article or poem occasionally but nothing like enough to satisfy the inexorable demands of a weekly paper. His own health was anything but robust. A friend described him as having a dyspeptic appearance, and contrasted the strength of his mind with the weakness of his body. The two blows he had sustained had strained him for a time, filling his mind with darkness, and then with a craving for renewed labour. Like a general when a campaign begins, he was immediately in action, planning, suggesting or negotiating; his manner frank, short and decided. He employed John Mitchel, a Northern attorney, who had contributed a volume to the shilling a copy *Library of Ireland* series that Duffy was producing to offset the intellectual stagnation of the time, to be *The Nation's* manager

and later made him the chief leader writer. He also brought
over from London a trained journalist whom he had
known as a schoolboy. This was Thomas D'Arcy McGee,
whom he rated as the most gifted of the Young Ireland
poets after Mangan and Davis. Other men who came into
the movement " in the day of disaster, almost of desperation " were Thomas Francis Meagher and Richard
O'Gorman. With Mitchel and McGee these formed the
backbone of what Duffy called the second Young Ireland
Party and their considerable debating power lent it excep-
tional strength.

Davis's death profoundly affected Duffy's career. Before
this time the life he had lived, despite its close connexion
with public agitations of the day, was essentially a journalist's life, and the student side of him found platform work
and exhibitionism of any kind distasteful. He was now com-
pelled, willy-nilly, to give up such time as he had previously
devoted to reading and reflexion, and to pass his life in the
fever and tumult of political action. Somebody was needed
to succeed Davis as the recognised leader of the group but,
though Duffy was the senior member available, he neither
then nor later ambitioned that role. Instead he used his
influence to promote Smith O'Brien into that position
despite the common criticism of his formal manners and
English accent in which it was said there was too much of
the Smith and not enough of the O'Brien. Duffy wanted to
see the group continuing to make a broad appeal. In particular he was anxious to avoid a drift to the left or the
adoption of any policy that might alienate the propertied
classes from them, and he told O'Brien that as a man of
property himself and a Protestant he could best achieve this.
The men of property, he felt, would not listen to young
men who were mostly Catholics and sprung from the trading
classes. O'Brien had hitherto been a neutral, neither an Old
Irelander nor a Young Irelander and had been O'Connell's

loyal deputy and a peacemaker among the conflicting elements. He had been the intimate friend of Davis and now became a close ally of Duffy, agreeing with him about the need to be watchful for any ultra-democratic and ultra-Catholic tendencies. O'Brien was older than any of the Young Irelanders and had the advantage over them of having a seat in the House of Commons. His selection had the effect of making Duffy a sort of deputy leader, an informal position which he continued to discharge from his editor's office in D'Olier Street which continued to be the Young Ireland workshop and meeting place.

The policy of the group was as always to support O'Connell in the pursuit of repeal, but increasingly they distrusted the old man, however much he insisted that repeal was written on his heart. Two important developments hastened the disruption of relations. First, when O'Brien found himself a prisoner in the Palace of Westminster and deserted by the O'Connells for an act of defiance of Parliament which they had instigated, and, secondly, when O'Connell allied himself with Russell to defeat the Tories under Peel and to put a Whig Government in office. This, the Young Ireland group feared, would lead to the undue deferment of the major national objective and its possible abandonment even in exchange for lesser favours including a share of patronage appointments. These appointments duly came, and O'Connell rejected an effort on the Young Irelanders' part to challenge the unopposed return to Parliament of Richard Lalor Shiel the member for Dungarvan on his becoming the Master of the Mint. For the time being, however, a major clash was avoided, and when it came, it was on the issue of the place of physical force in their affairs.

Duffy put Mitchel in temporary control of *The Nation* in 1846 and went into lodging in the hills above Dublin in order to complete in solitude a book on the Rising of 1641, a period that always fascinated him, that he had promised the *Library of Ireland.* The work was never finished. He had to turn away from it to save the *Library* from threatened financial collapse, and to deal with labour trouble that arose in connection with the printing of *The Nation.* But more disturbing were the complaints he began to receive about Mitchel. Wallis, one of Davis's most trusted friends, accused him of dealing with financial questions with appalling recklessness, and with foreign politics in a way that invoked the laughter of experts. John O'Hagan and Pigot, whose opinions Duffy was readier to accept, protested against the increasingly violent tone of the paper. In an article on the Sikhs Mitchel spoke of the blow which was to destroy the English Empire in the East as likely to be struck, "nearer home". "Heaven and earth," cried O'Hagan, "what is the meaning of this? With about as much prospect of achieving liberty by arms as of bringing Stonehenge to the Curragh why is the paper vapourising in this way? Besides the character it gets us which materially lessens our utility in other things, it is *suggestio falsi* to our own people and calculated to mislead and confuse them." He called on Duffy to take over immediately from Mitchel, and to busy himself with the issue of the Famine which was destroying the country, and with the practical steps for dealing with it. Duffy first contented himself, however, with reminding Mitchel that insurrections were not made to order in the back office of a newspaper. They were in the year 1846, not 1843. They had not the priests with them as they had then, nor perhaps the people. And where were the military leaders with skill and knowledge for such an enterprise as Mitchel had apparently in mind?

4

Before Duffy resumed editorship serious trouble erupted over what became known as the railway article in *The Nation*. A Government newspaper had suggested that, in order to deal with food riots which the developing famine had caused, the agitation for repeal should be regarded as treasonable, Conciliation Hall closed, and troops sent into the troubled spots by the railways that had just been constructed. Mitchel replied that if the railways were so used the people should fill up the cuttings and level the embankments. It might be useful, he wrote, to promulgate throughout the country, to be read by the repeal wardens in their parishes, a few short and easy rules for dealing with the railways in case the enemy made hostile use of them. Duffy did not quarrel with the substance of this, but he saw that Mitchel had erred tactically in associating the Repeal Association with his threat. This was playing into O'Connell's hands.

Mitchel saw his mistake and sought to remedy it, but O'Connell brought the matter up at the next meeting of the Association and insisted that the safety of the organisation was endangered by rash counsels of this kind, and that he must dissociate himself publicly from them. The Government also moved, charging Duffy with seditious libel; but neither this nor O'Connell's anger prevented him from publishing a leading article in which he justified the railway article and defended Mitchel. In doing so he was supported by Smith O'Brien and other prominent members of the party. O'Connell pressed his point. He sent for Duffy and Mitchel, and asked for an assurance that *The Nation* would not oppose the decisions of the Association;

otherwise he would have to disconnect the Association from
the paper. Duffy assured him that no one could be more
anxious to act habitually with the Association than they
were; they would not seek a quarrel, but they reserved the
right to consider the future decisions of the Association on
their merits. O'Connell thereupon took the matter to the
committee, and after a strenuous debate, action was begun
to ensure that *The Nation* would be kept out of the Repeal
reading rooms.

The result of Duffy's trial which began on the 16th July,
1846, seemed a foregone conclusion. With Blackburne,
the subtle and vindictive Chief Justice presiding, conviction was certain. But Robert Holmes, the brother-in-law
of Robert Emmet, now approaching his 80th year, split the
jury with a defence speech which the Judge said had never
been surpassed in a court of justice, and Duffy went free.
The news was received throughout Ireland with what Duffy
called a paroxysm of joy. " I wish," said O'Brien, " we
could have such language in Conciliation Hall as Mr.
Holmes is not ashamed to utter in the Queen's Bench."
Holmes had argued that Ireland was being treated as a conquered country, yet the people of a country so treated had
certain natural rights, including the right to resist the use
of force to stifle public opinion and these were precisely the
rights that were being insisted upon in the railway article.
With O'Connell in the chair, the Association thanked
Holmes for his speech, and sought his permission to print
and circulate it at their expense. They also voted to pay
Duffy's costs out of the Association's funds but Duffy
declined the offer as he declined similar offers in other
actions in which he was involved.

Before the Whigs assumed office in the summer of 1846,
and with Duffy's sedition trial pending, Russell attacked
The Nation, accusing it of giving expression to the ideas of
a party which excited every species of violence, which

looked to disturbance as its means and regarded separation from England as its end. Duffy described this outburst as calumnious and its imputations false but he regarded it as humiliating to defend the journal in public and did not do so. With his colleagues, however, he continued to assail the Whig alliance and to repeat that the Repeal policy was in danger. He believed that O'Connell the emancipator, guide and father of his people, was, in his old age, and under the influence of his feeble and malicious son, about to make a wreck not only of himself but of the cause to which he was pledged and of the people who loved him so tenderly but O'Connell denied this in every mood and tense. Repeal was still their goal but that should not prevent them from squeezing the government to do other things that would be of social and economic benefit to the country. Meanwhile he took steps to bring Young Ireland to heel. He called upon the Association to adopt a resolution outlawing the use of physical force in every circumstance. Anyone who refused to accept this doctrine would cease to be a member. " I do not accept," O'Connell said, " the services of any man who does not agree with me in theory and in practice."

The Young Irelanders consulted among themselves and decided to avoid the snare that had been laid for them by not retiring from the Association whatever resolutions were adopted. They also determined to deny as distinctly as possible any intention of violating the rules of the Association or of using it for any but peaceful purposes, and Mitchel actually declared that, as constitutional agitation was the very basis of the Association, nobody who contemplated any other method of bringing about the independence of the country had a right to attend there or to consider himself a fit member. By this means, if boldly, honestly and steadily carried out, legislative independence could be won; and with this conviction, he should feel it

his duty, if he knew any member who, either by speaking
or writing, attempted to incite the public to arms or violence as the method of obtaining their liberty, while that
Association existed, to report such member to a committee
and move his expulsion. He personally entertained no
thought of resorting to violence. Peace was their only true
policy, their only policy and would be if they did not
wantonly ruin it, their inevitably successful policy.

This and other statements in the same vein carried no
conviction to O'Connell, and John at a meeting in his
father's absence insisted that the resolution must be adopted
unequivocally, and, if by any chance, the resolution were
rejected, the Liberator and his friends would leave the
Association for ever. In these circumstances, O'Brien walked
out of the meeting and was followed by the Young Irelanders ; so that on what seemed at the time a rather
theoretical point the break occurred that they had determined to avoid. Within a couple of years, however, the
issue proved to be anything but theoretical.

This strategic victory for O'Connell was seen by Duffy's
correspondents as having been brought about in part by
churchmen. His Kilkenny friend, Dr. Robert Cane, told him
that it was the result of the prearranged blackening of
the Young Irelanders' characters in the minds of the
Catholic clergy ; in his area they were regarded as little
better than infidels and most inimical to the Church ; and
elsewhere it was largely the same story. The Bishop of
Ardagh gloried in the fact that in his diocese there were no
physical force men nor, thank God, any schoolboy philosophers, false and sanguinary repealers, or Voltairian
repealers. *The Nation* was the most dangerous publication
that ever appeared in Ireland and had been ignominiously
expelled from almost all their literary institutions. Duffy,
towards the end of his day, could assert, however, that all
these schoolboy philosophers, after spotless lives, had died

in the faith ; while the opinion of bishops on political questions, once so valuable, had no longer force or character.
But Young Ireland had clerical friends too, even in the
episcopacy. Dr. McGinn, the Bishop of Derry, who had a
high regard for Duffy, sent the Association resolutions
adopted by his clergy, the principal one containing a reservation identical with that made by the Young Irelanders on
the peace resolution. Another northern bishop appealed to
the Association to recall the seceders, but to no avail. And
Fr. C. P. Meehan—though this might have been expected—
also remonstrated against the treatment of *The Nation* and
the enforced retirement of Smith O'Brien from the Association. For his pains, however, he was told that he too had
ceased to be a member as he did not acquiesce in the principles on which the Association was based.

Duffy received letters from the country asking him to
make a stand against " this corrupt and disastrous tyranny "
and, fearing misunderstanding, he explained the policy of
the Young Irelanders in *The Nation*. " It is not to conciliate
our accusers we exercise forbearance—not to get this journal
taken once more into favour—emphatically we say that *The
Nation* can do without Conciliation Hall better than Conciliation Hall can do without *The Nation*—but because we
should feel the sin and shame lie heavy on our own souls if
we were conscious that we had done an act or written a
word to perpetuate or exasperate these mad quarrels. Better
that *The Nation*, and all who contributed to it, were sunk
in the Red Sea than that they should become the watchword
of faction, the pretext of division, the rock whereon to
make shipwreck of so noble a cause." But the campaign
against them continued, and *The Nation* already banned
from the Repeal Reading Rooms, was publicly denounced
by O'Connell in terms which Duffy described as a denial
and denunciation of all Robert Holmes had argued so successfully in the railway prosecution. The result was that

within a few months the Repeal Association became a
wilderness. The remonstrances that poured into Conciliation
Hall were ignored but Duffy published them in *The Nation*
and opened a special section of the paper under the title
of *Phalanx* to discuss the issues that were at stake. These
communications O'Connell stigmatized as being in the tradition of the infidel philosophers who launched the French
Revolution, while his son caused a remonstrance to be flung
into the gutter that was tendered by more than half of
Dublin's repeal wardens and fourteen hundred other
repealers. This led to a protest meeting in the Rotunda, at
which Father Kenyon, one of *The Nation's* writers, whilst
striving as the Young Irelanders always did, to distinguish
O'Connell's personal character from what went on in Conciliation Hall, renounced his leadership until he mended his
ways. O'Connell countered this much-publicised occasion
by bringing a bishop into Conciliation Hall to protest
solemnly against the Young Irelanders who, he said, had
failed in their attempt to sever the ties which united the
clergy and laity. Duffy joined issue with the bishop, inviting
him to give at least one instance in which *The Nation* had
preached infidelity or had endeavoured to separate the
priests from the people. There was no reply. Then the
Young Irelanders held a mass meeting in the Rotunda,
attended not only by the seceders but by a number of the
more solid and middle class repealers, at which two priests
from the Dublin diocese defended the young men against
the attack on their religious position.

Duffy availed of an opportunity he got somewhat later to
explain where he stood personally. " I for one," he said,
" would purchase neither knowledge nor freedom at the
sacrifice of religion. Man's relation to God is the most
serious question he can ever have to determine ; and no
human liberty, or glory or prosperity, ought to come in
competition with it. If a word would make this island a

proud nation, renowned from pole to pole, but a nation without religion, God forbid that I should pronounce it." " The policy of a rising nation," he said on another occasion, " ought to be as grand and comprehensive as the sublime system of the Catholic Church which, *pace* Macaulay, finds in its bosom a place and a work for every class of intellect and disposition." The work to be done by Young Ireland was " to gather new friends, to convert ancient enemies, to remove hereditary prejudices, to make the past plain by the light of history, the future by the light of political science , , , and to elevate and inform the popular will, that true moral force which is destined to work our deliverance."

Impressed by the reaction in favour of the seceders, O'Connell, at the next meeting of the Association, moved to close the ranks in face of the growing famine in the country. Let the Young Irelanders, he said, show that they give up everything contrary to law and he would concede everything that the law would permit. He proposed a conference with Smith O'Brien, but O'Brien would not come to Dublin and haughtily told an O'Connell emissary that he had no intention of debating peace resolutions which were merely a pretence for getting rid of troublesome members of the Association. This was an attitude with which the seceders in general did not agree, and Duffy with Dillon and James Haughton availed of an opportunity for meeting O'Connell. The interview was a failure from the start. O'Connell told them that it was melancholy to think that the Repeal Association had to negotiate with the compositors' room of a newspaper office and he refused to look at the letters Duffy had brought with him from forty districts where secessions had taken place specifying the terms on which they would be willing to return to the fold. It was all over, O'Connell said; the Association would work on its way as best it could despite the paltry machinations of the Little Ireland gang. What sins had the Association

committed that it should be condemned and handed over to
such executioners as Duffy, Mitchel and the Young Irelanders?   He would rather see it emptied of the last man
than submit to their dictation.

With re-union out of the question, the seceders formed
in January, 1847, what they called the Irish Confederation,
a development which D'Arcy McGee credited to Duffy
primarily.   " Duffy projected the Confederation," he said.
" He made it.   He won over all the considerable men who
joined it, one by one, by dint of argument and exhortation.
He gave it its impulses and policy.   He was the Confederation."   He did this through his chairmanship of the organisation committee.   He prepared a programme for the formation of Confederate clubs in every parish in Ireland and
told them what they were to do.   They were to be what
would now be called pressure groups, bringing the force
of public opinion into play.   In the town they had special
duties; they were to encourage the use of Irish manufac-
ture, promote knowledge of the history and resources of
Ireland, work for the extension of popular franchise and
procure attendance at lectures and classes of youths of ten
years upwards so that they might learn the history of their
country which was being kept from them in the National
schools.   They were also to seek signatures to addresses to
the Queen stating the rights of Ireland and calling for the
re-assembly of an Irish Parliament.   The country clubs were
given special duties also directed towards procuring full
recognition and protection of the rights of the tenant-farmer
and the labouring classes, and were to diffuse knowledge
about agriculture and discourage secret societies.   For all
clubs whether in the towns or country Duffy had this injunc-
tion : they were to pursue their labours in love and charity
so as to promote harmony among all Irishmen.   They were
therefore to ask Protestants for their help but, he said,

" when you ask them, if you do not mean to protect the religious liberty of Protestants in all contingencies as zealously as you would protect your own, you are hypocrites, unworthy of liberty ".

These political developments, it should be remembered, took place in a country that from 1845 onwards was suffering a calamity unparalleled in its history. Famine, disease and death were rampant as a result of a potato blight that first put in an appearance in Ireland in the month in which Davis died. The remedies that were devised to deal with this situation were utterly and hopelessly inadequate, based as they were on an ignorance of Irish conditions and on a rigid economic and social theory implemented by an equally rigid governmental machine directed by the British Treasury from Whitehall. It has been well said that the English despite the fact that they had been so long in the country knew less about Ireland than they did of the distant parts of the Empire. The Confederation, through their local clubs, counselled the farmers in 1847 to hold the harvest till the needs of their own families were supplied, and this may have prevented some food leaving the country, but it did nothing to ease the situation in areas of greatest need where cooking any food other than the potato had become a lost art. O'Connell, sick and sore in spirit, and seeing the membership of his Association dwindle from millions to a mere handful and the Repeal movement he had created disintegrate, tried to bring the House of Commons to an appreciation of what was happening in Ireland but could raise little more than a pathetic whisper. Then, on the advice of his doctors, he took himself to the Continent where he died, the greatest popular leader, in Gladstone's opinion, the world had ever seen, a statesman who never for a moment changed his end and never hesitated to change his means. His death, in May, 1847, caused a startling revulsion of opinion which manifested itself in the General Election that was held that summer. In the towns the Confederates held whatever support they had accumulated, but such popularity as they had achieved was forgotten in a moment in the rural areas. The people of Munster flew into a mad rage believing that the Young Irelanders had killed their leader. Only two Confederate members—Smith O'Brien and another—were returned; the rest were annihilated; and the wild Father Kenyon was with difficulty rescued by brother priests from the violence of the Limerick mob.

5

The trouble with the Confederates was their inability to agree on a common policy and their extraordinary preoccupation with plans that could yield no short-term benefit. People were dying or emigrating in hundreds of thousands, yet O'Brien looked to the land-owning gentry of whom he was one to declare themselves for self-government which he believed they would do if their fear of democracy could be allayed, while John Martin tried to woo the Presbyterians of Ulster. But what was wanted, the others thought, was immediate control of the national resources. It was at this stage that a hitherto unknown man, lame, deaf and near-sighted, James Fintan Lalor, wrote to Duffy, outlining in startling original terms his plan for associating the land problem with that of national independence. He held that beside the land, repeal was a petty parish question; a fight for the land would unite North and South. But the fight could not be waged unless the Young Irelanders abandoned the pledges they had given to employ only legal means in the prosecution of their rights. " As regards the use of none but legal means," he wrote, " any means and all means might be made illegal by Act of Parliament; and such pledge, therefore, is passive obedience. As to the pledge of abstaining from the use of any but moral force, I am quite willing to take such pledge, if, and provided, the English Government agree to take it also; but if not, not." In another letter he made it clear that he did not advise insurrection in a form in which the Irish could not hold their own against the army of occupation. The small farmers and farm labourers would never wield a weapon in favour of repeal; they could, however, be relied upon to carry out a policy of Moral Insurrection, of disobedience to selected laws, and he proposed that they should begin by withholding their rent.

The letters, which Duffy circulated, made a profound impression on the Confederates and especially on John Mitchel and Father Kenyon, but Smith O'Brien was of the firm opinion that the doctrines enunciated in them would dissipate all hopes of winning any section of the gentry. Seeing, therefore, the growing unlikelihood of agreement on a policy, he made it known to Duffy that he would be happier if he could retire altogether from politics. Duffy, who had been instrumental in placing O'Brien at the head of the movement and who continued to be his mentor, insisted that there was no course for any of them but an onward one. If they could not agree on a programme for the famine, they could at least proceed to formulate a plan for restoring the Irish Parliament, which was common ground with them all. O'Brien was asked by the Council of the Confederation to prepare a forward-looking policy along these lines, but his draft, when it came along, was considered unsatisfactory. Duffy was a principal critic of it. It was, in his opinion, not specific ; what they wanted was a rational answer to give to practical but timid people who asked *how* they meant to repeal the Union. It was not enough to prepare the public for action and leave them there.

The natural upshot of this criticism was that Duffy himself was asked to prepare a plan. While he was thus engaged Mitchel almost overnight made up his mind that Lalor was right and the two of them with Father Kenyon then declared that the Confederation and *The Nation* should pronounce for Lalor's policy. This change of front was, understandably, ill-received by the Council and Duffy, Dillon, and O'Hagan in particular were convinced that Mitchel was going to destroy himself and probably the Confederate cause as well. They strove hard, therefore, to make him change his mind but to no avail. And while their negotiations were continuing, Mitchel tried Duffy's spirit sorely by stating in leading articles for *The Nation* opinions which Duffy said Mitchel knew he would never sanction. In one of them he defended the perpetual slavery of the negro, and in another he objected to the emancipation of the Jews. Duffy struck out the objectionable passages and then made it known to Mitchel and Lalor that while they could advocate their opinions in *The Nation* in letters over their own signatures they would not be permitted to do so in leading articles or literary criticism. Mitchel met this situation by establishing a paper of his own, *The United Irishman,* to which he gave Tone's motto that if the men of property would not help the national cause, recourse would be had to the men of no property. The paper boldly and defiantly advocated Lalor's policy and attracted wide attention. Thus came a separation of Duffy and Mitchel after nearly three years of close association. In parting, Mitchel gave Duffy credit for having always acted on good and disinterested motives, with the utmost sincerity, and with uniform kindness to himself personally. Duffy duly presented his report to the Confederation on the way and means of obtaining an independent Irish Parliament. Could the thing be done at all, he asked, and, if so, how and when? Certainly, no short cut or dramatic solution could be expected. Since the death of O'Connell, there was no *authority* in Ireland recognised by the whole nation. A national movement to succeed would have to recreate such an authority, beginning with a small nucleus of able, honest and devoted men from which such a power would grow. They would win authority in the most legitimate way by deserving it. The first condition of success was that they should be governed not only by fixed principles but by a scheme of policy carefully framed and worked out in detail. The sudden explosion of an outraged people had sometimes given liberty to a nation, he argued, but mere turbulence or agitation, with no definite scheme of action,

never. The Repeal Association was a disastrous example, a
great steam power which turned no machinery.

What was first wanted was a Parliamentary Party: not
necessarily a large one, for even a score of Irish members of
capacity and character could effectually use the House of
Commons to teach all Europe to understand the iniquity of
English Government in Ireland. This course would not only
revive the sympathy of foreign nations, but win that of just
Englishmen, and gain the trust of the Irish people by effec-
tual work done on their behalf. Such a Party could rule the
House of Commons, divided as it was, and led by weak
Party leaders. There had never been such an Irish Party in
the British Parliament, and Duffy insisted that it would not
be by consent of the Parliament, but in spite of it, not by
its grace and favour but because of its utter impotence
against claims of Justice, vigorously asserted, that they would
succeed. The Irish Party must be kept pure and above suspicion by a pledge never to ask or accept favours for themselves and others from any Government, and must exhibit
no preference between Whig and Tory. Whoever could help
Ireland were their friends. Such a Party encamped within
the walls of Parliament would be " more formidable than
armed insurrection ".

At home the Confederates could labour to secure the election to corporations and boards of guardians of men of
trust, intelligence and perseverance, and use these representative bodies as local Parliaments, supplying as far as possible by counsel and guidance the existing want of a legislature. Ireland had never since 1782 put forth systematically
the power that lies in the awakened public spirit of a
nation to help itself. If that power were wisely used, hurting
no Irish interests, some of the grand juries could be won to
the same views as they had held in 1843. Ulster would probably follow, for with the North nationality was only a question of time and security.

Once the representatives in Parliament had made the case of Ireland plain to all men, and had established that they were the undoubted spokesmen of the nation, then it would be their right and duty to stop the entire business of the House of Commons till the Constitution of Ireland was restored. From such a position there seemed but two outlets—the Irish demand would be conceded or the Irish representatives would be forcibly ejected, in which event they would fall back upon the organised people whom they represented. They would return to Ireland where a great Council of the Nation would be convened consisting of all the elected representatives, both parliamentary and local. Such a Council would naturally demand the restoration of the Irish Parliament. A like demand was conceded in 1782 and Duffy believed it would be again conceded if it became undeniably a national demand. If not, a nation of seven millions united in a single purpose and guided by trusted counsellors, would know how to enforce their will.

The Council of the Confederation adopted Duffy's ideas by fifteen votes to six, the opposition being led by Mitchel and Thomas Devin Reilly, who put forward Lalor's plan as an alternative. The issue was then put to a public meeting of the Confederation, consisting mainly of young men, in a series of resolutions proposed by Smith O'Brien but possibly drafted by Duffy. These declared that the Council was established to attain an Irish Parliament by the combination of classes and by the force of opinion exercised in constitutional operation, and that no means of a contrary character could be recommended or promoted through its organisation while its fundamental rules remained unaltered. Mitchel moved an amendment declaring that the Confederation did not feel called upon to promote, or condemn, doctrines promulgated by its members in letters or speeches. The rules of the Confederation no doubt had said that its members were to attain their end by force of opinion, but what did

opinion mean? And should it be always legal, always
peaceful? Italy and Austria had been rescued by opinion
and sympathy, they were told, but it was opinion with the
helmet of a National Guard on his head, and a long sword
by his side ; it was opinion standing, match in hand, at the
breech of a gun charged to the muzzle. He had no faith in
a Parliamentary Party, and repeated attempts to obtain combination of classes had ended in failure.

John Pigot, Michael Doheny, P. J. Smyth and Thomas
D'Arcy McGee were among those who supported O'Brien's
resolutions. Mitchel wanted to stop payment of the Poor
Rate—this was a variant of Lalor's original proposal—but
O'Brien pointed out that the effect of this would be to deprive
the starving poor of their principal source of relief. Doheny
rejected Mitchel's policy because it lacked all possibility of
success. The peasantry had no arms but if they had, why
conceal the fact that the majority of them would use them
not for the Confederation but against it? Smyth reminded
the meeting that to rely on a single class, the men of no substance, would be to expose themselves to the mobs which
in Limerick and Belfast had assailed the Confederates. How
could even this class be reached? With the upper and
middle classes in hostility, as well as the priesthood, it
would be impossible by speaking or writing to induce a
single parish in Ireland to rise in insurrection. D'Arcy McGee
opposed the new policy, not because it was treason against
the law, he said, but because it was treason against commonsense. Mitchel had denied that he was for immediate insurrection, but how could he put it off if the Lord Lieutenant
proclaimed a district and ordered arms to be given up?
Were the men so incited to be left to their fate?

Here was the beginning of a schism that lasted down into
our own days, a schism that divided Young Ireland into a
republican minority that was prepared to resort to force to
achieve its goal, and a majority that, through constitutional

action, though not closing the door to the contingency of revolutionary action in certain circumstances, sought an independent parliament but under the English King who would also be King of Ireland. Mitchel left the Confederation accompanied only by Reilly, when his amendment was defeated by 317 votes to 188. His former friendship for Duffy was replaced by a bitterness which grew enormously with the passage of time. This showed itself in flaming words that burned into the mind of the sensitive Duffy and made him miss no opportunity of retaliating. Mitchel, as a result of this controversy, he wrote, was " the most disabled and discredited politician in Ireland. He had pluck, men said, and rhetorical power, but not a tittle of the supreme faculty which estimates forces accurately, and encounters difficulties successfully, called in its modest form good sense ".

The second part of that statement was true but the majority of the Confederate leaders were to demonstrate that they too were supremely lacking in commonsense. They certainly failed to estimate accurately the forces on which they could rely and those ranged against them, and they allowed themselves to be overwhelmed emotionally by the situation that confronted them on the abdication of Louis Philippe and the proclamation of the new French Republic. This occurred in February, 1848, within a month of Mitchel's secession from the Confederation.

6

The wave of sympathy with France that swept over the world, and that encouraged oppressed peoples elsewhere to revolt, affected Ireland profoundly. The French were Ireland's ancient allies and had offered officers and men less than five years earlier to lead an Irish revolt. Now they were raising once more aloft the torch of freedom for Ireland to grasp, or so the Confederation thought. When the news reached Dublin, Duffy was separated from his principal colleagues who were down in Waterford contesting a bye-election for which Meagher was their candidate. On his own initiative Duffy rhetorically asked a meeting of the Confederation what they ought to do. It seemed to him, he said, that they had no honourable choice. In the recent controversy with Mitchel he had voted against rash words and rash courses but he had declared that he would embrace any chance of fighting for Ireland in which not a class but the country, Old Irelanders and Young Irelanders, Protestant and Catholic, gentry and labourer, could unite ; and now the occasion had come, or it would never come in their lifetime. And in the next issue of *The Nation* he declared that Ireland's opportunity, thank God and France, had come at last. Its challenge rang in their ears like a call to battle, and warmed their blood like wine. They had to answer the challenge, if they were not to be slaves for ever. "We must unite," he cried, " we must act, we must leap all barriers but those which are divine: if needs be, we must die, rather than let this providential hour pass over us unliberated."

He urged his friends as they returned to town, to end the feud among Nationalists and to get ready to act quickly in concert with the countries on the Continent which every

day's papers indicated were rising to end misgovernment.
A conference with the Old Irelanders was arranged; Duffy
undertook to move in the Confederation that Mitchel and
his supporters would be invited to return; and at Dillon's
suggestion, he also undertook to seek an agreement with
Mitchel on ways and means of attaining their goal. O'Brien,
reluctant leader that he was, was delaying coming back to
Dublin from Clare as he wished the Confederates independently to choose their own course, but Duffy urged him to
return without delay in a letter that showed that he shared
O'Brien's preoccupation with the problems of class and his
horror of mob law. Any doctrine which led the labourers
to regard their interest as the only honest one was in fact as
selfish and fraudulent as the worse dogmas of despotism.
" There will be an outbreak sooner or later," he told O'Brien,
" be sure of that, but unless we provide against it, it will be
a mere democratic one, which the English Government will
extinguish in blood. Or if, by a miracle, it succeeds, it will
mean death and exile to the middle as well as the upper
classes. As Ireland lies under my eye now I see but one
safety for her—a *union* of the Old and Young Irelanders,
an arraying of the middle class in front of the millions, and
a peaceful revolution, attained by watching and seizing our
opportunity. By peaceful I mean without unnecessary or
anarchical bloodshed. It may be won without a shot being
fired. But trust me, if there is no such junction, and if things
are let to take the course they are tending towards, we will
see the life of the country trampled out under the feet of
English soldiers, suppressing a peasant insurrection; or you
and I will meet on a Jacobin scaffold ordered for execution
by some new Marat or Robespierre, Mr. James Lalor, or
Mr. somebody else. It is the fixed and inevitable course of
revolutions when the strength of the middle classes is permitted to waste in inaction.

If you want a graphic picture of it read Lamartine's

History of the Girondists, and you will see how Smith
O'Brien had to fly the country. Mr. Meagher was ordered
for execution, Richard O'Gorman died of starvation in trying to escape the guillotine ; M. J. Barry heard his own
Hymn of Freedom chanted by his pursuers ; T. D. McGee
was piked, John Dillon massacred and John Pigot killed
himself in horror and despair. History reproduces itself. We
may have a peaceful and happy revolution, and Ireland's
opportunity is coming fast ; but much depends on you. If
you make such a junction and return to Ireland, we will
probably have another '82 in 1849 ; if not, God shield the
country."

O'Brien was as optimistic as the rest of them. He told
the Confederation at their next meeting that while he had
never promised speedy success the end was within view. Dis-
cretion was however indispensable; if an outbreak took place
at present the Government would put it down in a week. He
made proposals for uniting all repealers and for fraternising
with the French people. He spoke of a deputation to the
United States and the formation there of an Irish Brigade
as the nucleus of an Irish Army. But when Duffy and company urged on him the necessity of obtaining arms, money
and a few trained soldiers from France or America, O'Brien
asked for patience ; he was persuaded that a section of the
gentry, large enough to complete the national character of
the movement, would declare for self-government, but he
could not invite gentlemen to do so if they had entered into
negotiation to commit high treason. On the other hand
Mitchel told Duffy when they met that there were arms
enough in the country already, and that the people must find
their own leaders. All the people needed was a prize worth
fighting for, and he would show them such a prize by proposing to found an Irish Republic. Never, Duffy commented
later, was a man so metamorphosed ; he used to be a modest
and courteous gentleman, now he demeaned himself as if the

French Revolution and the new opportunities it furnished were his personal achievements. Duffy and Dillon were appalled by this extravagance. To their way of thinking the French Revolution had not made Mitchel's proposal of a peasant war any more reasonable, and his suggestion, altogether unexpected, of a Republic would drive away the Old Irelanders friendly to reunion as effectively as his former policy had driven off the middle classes. However, Mitchel returned to the Confederation at the end of March, but this did not prevent him from following his usual independent line.

A deputation led by O'Brien went to Paris to congratulate the French Republic but failed to obtain even a declaration of sympathy; the British Foreign Office had seen to that. In their absence Duffy looked after the Confederates' affairs. He was unable, however, to control the extravagances of *The United Irishman* though O'Brien had asked him to try to do so, fearing as he did that Mitchel would ruin the cause of Repeal. One article of his which recommended that vitriol should be thrown on soldiers whenever a rising should take place was widely quoted in the English press. Excitement in Ireland mounted as it began to appear as if freedom could be had for the asking. The popular uprising in France had been followed by others equally successful in Austria and Germany. So that when O'Brien returned, he with Duffy and their close associates applied themselves immediately to the task of conciliating the divergent elements within the country in order to present a common front to the Government and the world. They were not very successful. A Protestant Repeal Association was founded with Samuel Ferguson at its head but all efforts to induce representative members of the Conservative Party to join it failed. They did not trust the Catholic masses. Duffy, one of them said, is no bigot, but he must know well that he could not find ten men of his

own creed in Ireland who would be as tolerant as himself.
He may be enthusiastic enough to believe it possible that he
and his handful of allies could protect religious liberty in a
Parliament of priest-selected members; but it is the dream
of an enthusiast. He and his friends would be the first
victims.

Meanwhile the Government was not idle. They prosecuted
a number of the Confederates for seditious speeches and
kept them all under close surveillance. According to the Prime
Minister, treason had never been so blatant in any country
as it was then in Ireland and the Government could not be
blamed for not being able to distinguish, as Duffy did,
between Mitchel's little group of fanatics who proclaimed
immediate and terrible war for a Republic but failed to
provide themselves with even a basket of cartridges, and
the majority who increasingly recommended the people to
arm in order to achieve a peaceful solution to their more
moderate aims. The Government had other and potentially
more dangerous troubles to contend with nearer home.
Under the influence of the events in Paris, the discontented
English workers had joined the Chartist movement in vast
numbers and, under the demagogic leadership of Fergus
O'Connor, threatened to overthrow the established order,
by force of arms if necessary. But O'Connor's move was
frustrated, as O'Connell's had been at Clontarf, when the
Government employed a large army of police, military and
special constables to prevent a march on London. Public
opinion rallied in their favour, and when Smith O'Brien ventured to explain to the House of Commons the significance of
the delegation he had led to Paris, he was shouted down by
the jubilant and disorderly Government Party. He returned
to Dublin convinced that there was no hope of a peaceful
arrangement with England, proposed to the Council of the
Confederation the formation of a National Guard, and then
set out on a tour of Munster.

Mitchel was one of the party assigned by the Confederation to accompany O'Brien, but O'Brien told him frankly that he could not appear upon the same platform with him without doing violence to his feelings. But when he got to Limerick, he found Mitchel there before him and was so deeply offended that he asked the organising committee to postpone the meeting. This they were not willing to do and the large Old Ireland element in the city which had hooted Mitchel on his arrival by the mail coach, not liking something he had written about John O'Connell, gathered outside the building in which the meeting was to be held, and attempted to set it on fire by burning an effigy of Mitchel close to the window. When that failed, they broke down the main door. O'Brien, in an effort to pacify the mob, was hit in the face by a stone, and incapacitated by a further blow in his side. Next day, greatly disfigured, he announced his intention of withdrawing altogether from public life.

No man was regarded at that time as so important to the cause as O'Brien and he was besieged with messages from all over the country asking him to reconsider his position. He agreed, however, to continue an active member of the Confederation only on condition that Mitchel and Reilly retired, which they immediately did. Duffy was among those to appeal to him. He did so through the medium of an article entitled *The Creed of the Nation* in which he " liberated his mind " and exposed himself to transportation which a recently enacted Treason Felony Bill had made the penalty for speaking and writing sedition. The article gave O'Brien extreme pleasure; he declared that he was fully prepared to hold himself, both morally and legally, responsible for the sentiments contained in it.

Duffy believed his *Creed* to be substantially the creed of the Irish Confederation. Liberty was their goal and was to be obtained peacefully if at all possible, but if not it would be obtained by the use of force. If it came by force it would come initially in the form of a Republic and would be welcomed as such; but, he would prefer a settlement by negotiation to a Republic won by insurrection, because insurrection would plant deadly animosities between men of the same Irish race; moreover, the sudden transition from Provincialism to Republicanism, passing through no intermediate stage, was an experience for which the Irish people were not ready. If an independent parliament, elected by the widest possible suffrage, were conceded with a Viceroy of Irish birth, they would defend such a settlement against all aggression either from without or from within. They would inevitably establish Tenant Right and abolish the Established Church, and they would compensate existing interests and settle the claims of labour. But one step further in the direction of revolution he did not believe they would go.

The Creed recounted the disaster that had recently overtaken Ireland. Other peoples had been protected from starvation because their rulers were of their own blood and race. In Ireland the revenue of three years was squandered in one, in ignorant and audacious experiments made in defiance of counsel and remonstrances from all classes of Irishmen. " The Prime Minister of England," he added, " . . . tells us that he will resist our joint claims for the management of our own affairs with the sword of the Empire. How can we answer but with the sword of Ireland? If famine has weakened the right arm of the people it has not paralysed His arm who rules the destinies of battles and fights by the side of the oppressed. Shall we tamely submit to see the last remnant of the Irish race and name sacrificed to the greedy and insolent spirit of English dominion? With God's blessing, no. We will sustain our natural right to this island against all enemies. All Ireland, from sea to sea, is arming and organising to uphold and enforce this right. The example of popular success throughout Europe, the threatening aspect of foreign nations, the sympathy of the English masses, and the triumphant justice of our cause may give us a peaceful victory. Heaven send it! But if not, my conscience is clear that we are able and entitled to take it. This is my belief. I seek no ingenious form of expression to shroud the naked thought. If we cannot save our country by peace, I am for war. And that we may save it by peace or war, I am for the universal arming and organisation of the people."

At this point in time there was no difference in their fundamental thinking as expressed in their papers between Duffy and Mitchel—they differed only as to methods—but Mitchel was the first to be arrested—on the 13th of May, 1848—under the new Treason Felony Act, and this development presented the Council of the Confederation with an urgent problem. They realised that no stone would be left unturned to secure a conviction against Mitchel leading to his transportation, so on the proposition of a minority of the members the question of rescuing him was examined. The result of the enquiries as summarised by Duffy, was far from encouraging. In Dublin city and county there were thirty Confederate clubs, numbering from one hundred to five hundred members each; the membership of clubs in other cities was of the same order; but in the countryside, despite what Lalor and Mitchel had assumed, there was not a solitary club; and the trampled peasantry were soon to show that without arms or training, they had not the guts for insurrection. On the other hand, the Government had ten thousand troops in Dublin, about forty thousand more in the country, and all the strategic points were guarded. There was not a week's supply of food in Dublin and, apart from growing crops, the rest of the country's supplies was in warehouses which an English army could easily destroy. But the chief difficulty of a rescue, according to Duffy, was Mitchel himself. He had scoffed at the necessity of systematic preparation and insisted that an emergency would produce its

own leader. But now that the need for action had arisen,
there were no trained men available, no arms worth talking
about, nor money to buy them. Meagher and O'Gorman
made a personal inspection of the Dublin clubs and arrived
at the conclusion that an attempted rescue, with people
unprepared, unorganised, unarmed and undisciplined, was
out of the question. O'Brien and Dillon had earlier convinced themselves that a rescue could not be undertaken
without ruin to the cause. The time was inopportune. It was
May and their idea was to wait until the Autumn, until the
harvest was in, when with the farm labourers able to leave
their employment, a union of parties perhaps achieved, and
money and arms secured, a general and simultaneous rising
could be embarked upon. In the upshot when, within a week
of his arrest, Mitchel was tried and convicted, he was allowed
to be carried off to penal servitude overseas without a hand
being raised to rescue him.

He was grievously disappointed, naturally. And so were
his close associates. One of them, Father Kenyon, came to
Duffy's house the next day along with T. B. MacManus to
demand what could be done. Duffy replied that the delay
in making preparations had nearly ruined their chances,
but they ought nevertheless to push ahead with the preparations that Mitchel had derided. They ought to send
to France for officers and men—presumably to the revolutionary clubs of Paris, for the government would have
nothing to do with them—and to America for officers and
money. MacManus promised that he would seize a couple
of the largest Irish steamers at Liverpool and load them
with arms and ammunition to be obtained from the army
depot at Chester Castle.

A meeting was arranged which Duffy, Dillon, John
Martin, Devin Reilly and Father Kenyon attended, and
there for the first time, attention was given to practical
measures for obtaining supplies of money, arms and officers;

and plans were laid for a diversion in England, in which
the Chartists had promised to co-operate. Smith O'Brien
was informed in general terms of the project. "It was,"
said Duffy, "a secret relief to men who loved him, and
made full allowance for the peculiar difficulty of his position, that they could take this risk wholly on themselves.
Enough was said to keep good faith; not enough to create
responsibility." About the same time, the long-delayed conference between Old and Young Ireland was held and
agreement was reached to dissolve both the Repeal Association and the Confederation and to replace them by a new
body to be known as the Irish League. The Confederate
clubs, however, were to remain in existence as the nucleus
of a National Guard and could arm themselves if they
chose. John O'Connell would have nothing to do with the
new organisation and it was whispered that he was being
used as a tool of Clarendon's to drive a breach between
the priests and the Confederates. Duffy gave him the
benefit of the doubt, however, on this score; his mind, he
said, was as unsteady as a quagmire and might have been
influenced by the latest events on the Continent which had
alienated the clergy and the middle classes everywhere and
had given the Government newspapers in Ireland a stick
to beat O'Brien, Duffy and company with. In June the
workers of Paris had overthrown the Republic they had
created only a few months earlier. The Archbishop of
Paris had been murdered in the course of a peace mission,
and in Italy a concession on the part of the Pope had been
rejected with scorn. The Government took advantage of
the wavering state of public opinion and began, rather
tentatively at first, to strike at the Confederates. They were
well informed. The proceedings in the clubs were open
and well-known to the police, and from April onwards a
man named John Donnellan Balfe who had been employed
by Duffy to help with the organisation of the National

Guard, kept Dublin Castle posted with particulars of the
Confederates' plans, differences and personal rivalries. And
the police made efforts by bribes, threats and falsehoods to
get men to testify against the Confederate leaders.   One
person they approached with offers of up to £500 was
Matthew Fannin, who had been in the same club as Duffy.
But he insisted that he had never heard Duffy uttering any
word incentive to war; on the contrary he had always
preached obedience to the law, without which he had said
no security could exist.   Fannin had heard Duffy say that
the men who advocated war were desperadoes, men of no
character whom he would not trust with sixpence, and as
for rifle clubs, they were nothing but fooleries.   But that,
as we have already seen, was not the whole story.

7

Duffy was the first to be apprehended and was committed to prison on a charge of publishing articles of a treasonable nature. It was on a Saturday evening, the 9th of July, 1848, that three detectives arrested him outside his house in the Dublin suburbs and took him off to Newgate, but not before he had taken leave of his family and given instructions to his wife for the secret disposal of important papers. Early in 1847, he had married his first cousin, Susan Hughes, a sister of Mrs. Margaret Callan, who later saw an edition or two of *The Nation* through the press while he was locked up. Susan was a highly cultivated woman who had studied music under Liszt and Chopin. Duffy himself had not a note, as the saying goes, nor were any of the children she bore him musical, but the task of raising them and of looking after her husband gave her little time to feel disappointed about their deficiencies.

For Susan he wrote "The Patriot's Bride", the nearest thing to a love-poem he ever wrote. The verses like the title show that their joint concern for the nation's well-being intertwined with their love-making so that the reader of today might well wonder which was the greater romance, ' To see the dank, mid-winter night pass like a noon' while they walked ' by Dodder's stream ' waking ' the old weird world that sleeps in Irish lore ', or remembering

> Tone's fiery hopes, and all the deathless vows
> That Grattan swore ;
>
> The songs that once our own dear Davis sang—ah me
> To sing no more.

The Nation office was simultaneously seized by the police and as the prison van containing Duffy passed by the office a crowd that had congregated there shouted " Take him out! Take him out!" D'Arcy McGee mounted the steps of the van and whispered to Duffy that they were going to rescue him but Duffy would have none of it. "No, no," he said, "a rescue will only be a street riot, unless we can take Dublin and hold it, and you know we can do neither. And we must wait for the harvest." The noisy crowd continued to obstruct the van until Duffy, at the instance of the police, appealed to them to be patient and to rely on their leaders.

The Governor of Newgate made Duffy as comfortable as he could in the long-condemned insanitary jail. He was able to get food from a nearby hotel and move freely among the other prisoners who had arrived. Among them were John Martin who had established *The Irish Felon,* to carry on the teachings of Mitchel's *United Irishman,* and R. D. Williams and Kevin O'Doherty who had jointly started another paper called *The Tribune.* He was allowed to have visitors as and when he liked ; and O'Brien and Dillon were among those who came to discuss the future lines of policy with him. And as *The Nation* and *Irish Felon* continued to appear, Duffy and Martin sent out their editorials from the jail. The prisoners had plenty of time to consider their personal predicament. The likelihood of a jury verdict in their favour was nil ; so they made no preparation for their defence. And as their property would pass to the Crown on their conviction they proceeded to divest themselves of whatever property they had. Duffy, for instance, auctioned his library and pictures in the interest of his family.

The first meeting of the Irish League was held within days of Duffy's arrest and a programme of organisation announced, but before they could meet again the Government tightened the security arrangements by directing a strict search for arms and by suspending the Habeas Corpus Act. They were now in a position to arrest and detain whomsoever they chose. This confronted the Confederate leaders who were at liberty with the choice of either allowing themselves to be taken or of banking on a premature rising without the help they sought from abroad. They decided to rise, an extraordinary decision for the situation was not materially different since Mitchel had called on the famished, apathetic population to strike for a republic, and Dillon sent the news in to Duffy. The Confederates were to seize Kilkenny and set up a Provisional Government there or, if that proved impracticable, to raise their followers in the neighbouring counties and to take the field. McGee was sent to Scotland to open up a channel through which it was believed arms and volunteers could be brought over to Ireland. Duffy and Martin were asked to pass the word on to the Dublin Confederates and other reliable persons. This they did through the staff of their journals whom they called into the prison. Some of these men urged that Dublin should not be omitted from the rising ; the fall of the Castle would be a certain stimulus to the country. Others more wisely said that the leaders should permit themselves to be arrested ; after a spell of imprisonment they would be able to resume preparations with a greater chance of success. But all debate ended when O'Brien accepted the plan which was brought to him from Dublin and announced his intention of leading the rising. " It was a spectacle strangely out of harmony with the sceptical scoffing generation in which it befell," Duffy wrote years later. " A gentleman of mature years, of distinguished lineage and station, the descendant of a great Celtic house, the husband of a charming wife, the father of a household of happy children, a man rich in the less precious gifts of fortune called opulence, staked his life to save his race from destruction. The chance of overthrowing the rooted power of the British Empire by insurrection was manifestly small, but a profound sense of public duty made him accept it

with all its consequences rather than acquiesce dumbly in
the ruin of his people."

Duffy, finding it increasingly difficult to carry on the paper
from his place of imprisonment, handed over the editorship
to his cousin and sister-in-law, Mrs. Callan (Margaret
Hughes). She was helped with a leading article, which someone said might have issued from the headquarters of a
National Army, written by the colourful Miss Elgee who
used the pen-name " Speranza ", and who was to be better
known later as the mother of Oscar Wilde. " In the name
of your trampled, insulted, degraded country ;"—the article
ran—" in the name of all heroic virtues, of all that makes
life illustrious or death divine ; in the name of your starved,
your exiled, your dead ; by your martyrs in prison cells and
felon chains ; in the name of God and man ; by the listening
earth and rocking Heaven, lift up your right hand to Heaven
and swear by your undying soul, by your hopes of immortality, never to lay down your arms, never to cease hos-
tilities, till you regenerate and save this fallen land." Duffy
managed to smuggle out an article that made a similarly
rousing appeal. Ireland was perhaps at that very hour in
arms for her rights, he wrote ; it was her last resource. They
were fighting because there was no remedy but the sword.
Neutrality was no longer possible. Men had to choose their
side, and quickly ; either to abandon liberty and join the
red ranks of England or to look for deliverance and glory
beneath the green banner of Ireland. The issue of *The
Nation* containing these calls to arms was ready for dispatch
when the police pounced upon the plant, seized the type and
arrested the staff. The other nationalist journals had already
received similar treatment.

For a whole week of indescribable anguish Duffy and his
fellow-prisoners were without news from Kilkenny. The
daily newspapers were silent ; and a messenger sent to
O'Brien failed to reach him. Escape was considered but

found to be impossible. And then, suddenly, word came
through of the inevitable disaster. Reilly came back to
Dublin in disguise and was seeking means of escape to
America. Doheny and MacManus were said to be in the
Galtees, and Meagher and Dillon in Waterford, vainly
striving to raise the country, while O'Brien, after making a
pitiful stand in Ballingarry, had been arrested. With
Dillon and Meagher he had gone through Kilkenny and
Tipperary urging the people to provide themselves with arms
and to be ready to rise. Crowds with " eyes red with rage
and desperation " greeted him everywhere but his immediate
object appeared obscure, and the priests going among the
people warned them against being led to the slaughter. They
dispersed and O'Brien found himself leading a few hundred
half-clad and wholly unarmed men on whom the police fired,
killing some and wounding others. All was over; and yet
worse was to come. " Many of the ignorant populace in
Dublin whispered that Smith O'Brien had deliberately
betrayed them and made a real insurrection impossible. The
police were probably responsible for this invention ; but Old
Ireland prejudice welcomed it, and it was for a time successful." "For the first and last time in my life," said Duffy, " I
flung myself down in despair, and declared that such an
insensate multitude could not be saved." That was in July,
1848. Three months later Duffy heard in Newgate that an
attempt was being made to lead the Dublin Confederate
clubs into an insurrection and that the Viceroy, Clarendon,
was to be seized. He sent out a message immediately. " I
utterly and unequivocally condemn and denounce any such
attempt. It would end in a massacre of the clubs, and afford
an excuse for hanging O'Brien. Whoever engages in it will
be committing a serious crime against the country. It may
even be a trap by another Dobbyn to betray the people to
the gallows. I beseech and entreat every Confederate who
regards my advice to set himself against it. I would rather

be hanged tomorrow than lend it the smallest countenance."
He also refused to have anything to do with a new journal
that Lalor suggested should be started to represent such
underground elements as remained in the post-Rising chaos.

O'Brien, Meagher, MacManus and Patrick O'Donoghue
were subsequently tried at the Clonmel Assizes and as they
awaited the verdicts they loudly sang the key verse of
Duffy's " Watch and Wait " :

> Brothers, if this day should set,
> Another yet must crown our freedom ;
> *That* will come with roll of drum,
> And trampling files, with *men* to lead them.
> Who can save
> Renegade or slave?
> Fortune only 'twines her garlands
> For the Brave !

They were sentenced to death but the sentence was remitted
later to transportation for life to Van Diemen's Land. Duffy's
fellow prisoners in Newgate fared relatively better. Williams
was acquitted by the connivance of the Crown Solicitor and
Kevin O'Doherty and Martin were transported for terms of
ten and fourteen years respectively. Duffy himself was the
last to be arraigned. He expected short shrift from Lord
Clarendon who he believed had conceived a personal dislike of him and had viciously directed all the moves for his
destruction, including the circulation of a slander that he had
thrown himself on the mercy of the Executive and would not
defend himself. At Clonmel, the Solicitor-General had
described Duffy as the " diabolical tempter who had ruined
the unfortunate O'Brien ", and a letter had been produced
that Duffy had sent O'Brien when he was about to embark
on the Munster meetings. This stated that while he knew
O'Brien had no desire to lead or influence others, there was

no half-way house for him now ; he was the head of the movement, was loyally obeyed and would have to shape out the course of the revolution. The revolution, however, was to be conducted with order and clemency or the mere anarchist would prevail with the people and the revolution would be a bloody one. If O'Brien had been found guilty of treason felony what hope was there for Duffy in the light of that letter?

He was brought to the bar of Green Street on the 8th of August on a charge of felony but, with the discovery of his letter to O'Brien, the Attorney-General announced that he could not permit the trial to proceed as he might find it necessary to substitute a charge of high treason. " I was sent back to prison," Duffy wrote later, " to prepare for death. For five months my fellow prisoners when we met in the ghastly prison chapel on a Sunday morning fancied that the public gallows, which forms its principal window, was destined to open for my last exit from that edifice."

D'Arcy McGee, who had escaped to America, summed up Duffy's character as if he were already dead. " All his life through he was a disciplinarian, an architect of systems. The teeming fertility of his mind was marvellous. Always and everywhere he was projecting some new move for Ireland. The large throbbing vein that descended from his forehead used to swell and blacken like an inky cord from the strain that events kept up under the power-wheels of his intellect. . . . In all he thought not one hair's breadth of selfishness." When he came to write his poem, " To Duffy in Prison ", however, McGee foresaw a different fate for him.

I saw once more the dome-like brow, the large and lustrous eyes,
I marked upon the sphinx-like face the cloud of thoughts arise,

I heard again that clear quick voice that as a trumpet
   thrill'd
The souls of men, and wielded them even as the speaker
   will'd—
I felt a cordial clasping hand that never feigned regard,
Nor ever dealt a muffled blow, or nicely weighed reward.
My friend! My friend!—Oh, would to God that you were
   here with me—
A-watching in the starry West for Ireland's liberty!

They will bring you in their manacles beneath their
   blood-red rag,
They will chain you like the conqueror to some sea-
   masted crag,
To their slaves it will be given your great spirit to annoy,
To fling falsehood in your cup, and to break your martyr
   joy,
But you will bear it noble, as Regulus did of old,
The oak will be the oak, and honoured e'en when fell'd;
Change is brooding over earth, it will find you mid the
   main,
And thronged between its wings you'll watch your native
   land again.

McGee so idolised Duffy that Dillon in May, 1849, said
that he was under pressure to attack McGee for writing as if
Duffy was the only man who had any intellect and that
O'Brien and Meagher were mere puppets in his hands.

On the 26th October, three days after the Clonmel
prisoners were sentenced, Duffy appeared in Green Street
for the second time. Only on the night before was he told
what the charge would be, and when the Court opened it
was found that, without notice to him, the Crown lawyers
had transferred him from the City of Dublin to the County
in order to improve the chances of finding a jury to convict

him. The Judges, "with lugubrious faces", were com-
pelled to direct that the trial could not take place in that
venue.

Duffy had put his general defence in the hands of Isaac
Butt, a burly bison-headed barrister who had begun to
manifest national sympathies, and of two juniors, Sir Colman
O'Loghlen and John O'Hagan, who were among his
own barrister friends.   This able combination blew
holes in the Crown case in the prolonged preliminary
skirmishes, and it was the 15th of February, 1849, before he
finally appeared before a jury and pleaded " not guilty ".   He
knew that no legal skill or oratorical power could save him
so long as the system of jury-packing continued; so before
that crucial point was reached, he drafted a notice to the
Attorney-General raising a doubt as to whether he would get
a fair trial and giving a detailed account of what had happened to the men who had been tried before him. This docu-
ment was widely publicised, and when Archbishop McHale
of Tuam suggested that the country should have an opportunity of pronouncing on the administration of the law, Dr.
Murray, a Professor of Theology at Maynooth, and a good
friend of Duffy's, prepared a remonstrance to the Lord
Lieutenant which secured more than forty thousand signatures, including men eminent in the Church and the profes-
sions. The Lord Lieutenant rejected the memorial, but Duffy
then " ventured to disturb the repose " of a man he knew of
old, Richard Lalor Shiel, who now held office in the Whig
Government but who had countered the packing of the juries
on the occasion of O'Connell's trial with Duffy and others in
1843. He also tried to stir up the conscience of the English
historian, Macaulay, with whom he had a slight literary
acquaintance and who was also a Cabinet Minister, by send-
ing him a copy of the jury panel prepared for the trial. This
included " the jeweller of the Lord Lieutenant, the hairdresser
of the Lord Lieutenant, his Excellency's shoemaker, the

chandler to the Chief Secretary, the bootmaker to the Com-
mander of the Forces, the engineer to the Drainage Commissioners, the cutler, grocer and purveyor to the Castle; the
saddler and seedsman of a former Lord Lieutenant, three
Government contractors, a compositor in the College Printing
Office, two vicars choral of St. Patrick's Cathedral, the
auctioneer to the Commissioners of Woods and Forests, and
the Consul of King Ernest of Hanover ". It is not apparent
what good, if any, these moves did; but when the actual jury
to try Duffy was empanelled the Government, to take the bad
look off it, felt obliged to include one safe Catholic among
them. The choice fell on Martin Burke, the proprietor of the
Shelbourne Hotel, who the Sheriff's officers were sure would
do their work; he was known to be a prudent man who had
never taken part in Catholic affairs. Butt, knowing Burke's
form, wanted to object to him but Duffy prevented him from
doing so, for the excellent reason that he had been so advised
by Mrs. Burke. She had called on Mrs. Duffy the night
before the trial to say that she and her daughter would be
sitting in the gallery facing the jury box and if her husband
went against Mr. Duffy, he might not return home! Burke
stood out for an acquittal—and, with the jury in disagreement, Duffy was put back for retrial.

At this point in the story, as he tells it, Duffy produces,
with understandable pride, a letter from John Martin, then
awaiting transportation in Richmond gaol, praising his plan
for resisting the main body of the enemy's force—his jury-
packers—and regretting that he and the others had not
followed the same line. " And though you know, Duffy,
that I am so unfortunate as to differ from you on many
points of policy, and upon at least one serious matter of
personal opinion, I am proud to acknowledge in you, after
glorious Davis, the father of the Irish National Party and
the chief writer of the party. But for *The Nation* which
your generous boldness and your fixedness of purpose and

your able pen have maintained for the last six years as our standard and rallying point of patriotism, every one of us —even Mitchel—would have remained in dull, hopeless obscurity." McGee rated Duffy even higher still : Davis, Mitchel and O'Brien and Meagher were, in his opinion, of the same class, but not of the same rank. When Davis died, who, he asked, was so fit to take his place as the friend who created it for him, and made way for him to fill it?

The retrial took place in April, 1849, nine months after Duffy's arrest. The jury was chosen from a list of special jurors, that is to say " the sons of peers, baronets and knights, magistrates, ex-sheriffs, grand jurors, squires, bankers, merchants and traders worth £5,000 " but they could not be got to agree as to whether the prisoner was guilty or not. Perhaps they had been influenced by the public remonstrance in favour of the prisoner, perhaps the persuasive talk of the defence lawyers had won them over, or perhaps they were just sick and tired of " The Queen against Duffy ". In any event they could not agree and were locked up for the night; and in the morning there was a majority of one in favour of an acquittal.

" And so," said Duffy, " I saw the daylight again. Among stalwart men whose manly faces were wet with tears, among dear friends who had made light in the darkness for me, I was led out of Newgate broken in health and fortune, but not broken in spirit, to take up again the hereditary task of our race and country." Among the good friends none had worked more arduously for him than John O'Hagan. Seeing that legal costs had completely beggared Duffy he sought ways and means of helping him as Father Mathew had earlier tried to do but Duffy would not allow a fund to be raised for his defence; the management of the Repeal Funds had created such disgust with the manipulation of public monies that he was resolved not to be the object of any pecuniary tribute what-

ever. O'Hagan was optimistic about the future. " For us,"
he told Dillon, " I have still great hopes of the country,
provided we succeed in saving Duffy. I cannot express how
much I feel to depend on that. Let him be free to direct his
labours to the reconstruction and proper direction of the
Young Ireland party, and that Lucas (the editor of *The
Tablet*) come here to give a right bent to the priests and we
will be better before the wind than ever. . . ."

Duffy had many messages from friends and colleagues.
O'Brien, who was awaiting transportation, sent him a farewell benediction. " My mind," he wrote, " is so overwhelmed with the multitude of topics connected with our
intercourse which arise to afford matter for reflection at a
moment such as this that I dare not allow my pen to record
my thoughts lest I should find myself unable to check its
career. It is enough for me to say that however painful to
both of us may have been the first results of that intercourse, my esteem for your character and my admiration
of your abilities remain unchanged.

Nor do I regard with any other feelings than those of
unmixed satisfaction the circumstances that you have been
more successful than I have been in resisting the power of
British Law. Both for your own sake and that of the
country I rejoice that it is your lot to remain in Ireland to
work for Ireland."

Dillon, from America, wrote : " Respecting the future, I
would only say, ' Would to God that I had one hour's talk
with you! The burden of my discourse would be—shun all
aristocratic alliances.' "

Carlyle, who had sent encouraging letters to Duffy while
in prison, saw a new and clearer course opening for him.
" You have," he wrote, " an Ireland *ready* to be taught by
you, readier by you just now than by any other man, and
God knows, it needs teaching in all provinces of its affairs,
in regard to all matters human and divine! Consider your-

self as a brand snatched from the burning, a *providential* man, saved by the beneficent Gods, for doing a *man's* work yet, in this noisy, bewildered, quack-ridden and devil-ridden world." And Carlyle's biographer saw Duffy at this point of time as the custodian of Ireland's opposition to the Castle and Downing Street, a rebel who could be neither coerced nor bullied nor bribed. " Respectable people " were expected to look askance at him, and at this crisis such countenance as Carlyle's company and friendship gave him was invaluable. The Castle resented this; and Carlyle showed Duffy a letter of private remonstrance he had received from the Lord Lieutenant. " It made no difference at all," Duffy said; " he stood by me steadily, and merely by doing so, did me immense good."

8

Following his release, Duffy toured the South and West of Ireland with Carlyle, and both of them subsequently described their experiences—Carlyle in a book which Duffy regretted was ever published, it was so mercilessly critical of unoffending persons whose hospitality Carlyle had accepted. Only Duffy and a few of his friends escaped his sarcasms. Carlyle frequently noted the enthusiastic reception Duffy got whenever he was " discovered ". In Dungarvan the whole population turned out and gazed at him " as if they would have stared thro' and thro' him ", and in Castlebar a young woman shyly thrust a bouquet, with a verse attached, into his hands. Over parts of their western journey a young man, blunt-nosed and of unextinguishable good humour, travelled in their company. This was one of the English Quakers who did so much for the Irish poor at this time. He was to be execrated thirty-odd years later when as Buckshot Forster he returned to Ireland as Chief Secretary. Duffy, in perhaps the finest passage he ever composed, described the region between Limerick and Sligo which bore everywhere the features of a recently conquered country. Clare was almost a wilderness, the ruined lands on the desolate shores of Lough Corrib showed that the destructive hand of man had been at work, between Killala Bay and Sligo every second house had been pulled down. " The degradation," he wrote, " which had fallen on the generous and spirited Celtic race was a sight such as I had nowhere seen or read of. The famine and the landlords have actually created a *new race* in Ireland. We saw on the streets of Galway crowds of creatures more debased than the Yahoos of Swift—creatures having only a distant and hideous resemblance to human beings. Grey-headed old men, whose idiotic faces had hardened into a settled leer of mendicancy, and women filthier and more frightful than the harpies, who at the jingle of a coin on the pavement swarmed in myriads from unseen places; struggling, screaming, *shrieking* for their prey, like some monstrous and unclean animals. In Westport the sight of the priest on the street gathered an entire pauper population, thick as a village market, swarming round him for relief. Beggar children, beggar adults, beggars in white hairs, girls with faces grey and shrivelled; women with the more touching and tragic aspect of lingering shame and self-respect not yet effaced; and among these terrible realities, imposture shaking in pretended fits to add the last touch of horrible grotesqueness to the picture! I saw these accursed sights, and they are burned into my memory for ever. Poor, mutilated and debased scions of a tender, brave and pious stock, they were martyrs in the battle of centuries for the right to live in their own land, and no Herculaneum or Pompeii covers ruins so memorable to me as those which are buried under the fallen rooftrees of an ' Irish Extermination ' ".

In the same summer Macaulay, writer and politician, spent a fortnight in Ireland and had similar experiences. In describing them, however, he was suavely philosophical whereas Duffy, in Carlyle's phrase, was " very plaintive with a strain of rage in his voice ". Race and class made all the difference in the approaches of the two men. "I cannot mend this state of things," Macaulay wrote, " and there is no use in breaking my heart about it." He was comforted in thinking, however, that between the poorest English peasant and the Irish peasant there was ample room for ten or twelve well-marked degrees of poverty. Political agitation was dead and buried; he had never seen a society apparently so well satisfied with its rulers, and the Queen on her recent visit had made a conquest of all hearts. The 1848 affair had caused

Victoria to regard the Irish as a terrible people and within
months of her coming to Dublin a mad Irishman had
attempted to take her life. Other Irishmen, almost as mad,
had concocted a plan to seize her and hold her as a hostage
in the Wicklow mountains, but Duffy, when he heard of
this, threw buckets of cold water on the idea. He had come
to see the futility, what has recently been rightly called the
tragi-comedy, of the 1848 enterprise.

The exterminations whose dire consequences Duffy and
Carlyle had seen were not confined to the West. Far from it.
In County Kilkenny, for instance, the Earl of Desart had
been an active exterminator, and had cleared out some five
hundred people since the commencement of the Famine
before two Catholic curates in Callan—Father Tom O'Shea
and Father Matthew Keeffe—decided it was time to call a
halt to his gallop. They formed a Tenant Protection Society
whose aims were to secure fair rents, tenant right as practised in Ulster, and employment. In a short time they had
many imitators, even in the North where rapacious landlords had begun to threaten the traditional Ulster custom.
Since 1846, an Ulster Tenant Right Association had been in
existence, and its leader, Doctor McKnight, who was the
editor of *The Banner of Ulster,* the official organ of the
General Assembly of the Presbyterian Church, was well
known to Duffy. He was, in his own words, " an old black-
mouthed Presbyterian " and the inheritor of Gaelic traditions.
He was passionately fond of the old melodies, many of
which in Irish he had heard from his father before Moore's
collections were heard of. Those streams of common interest,
North and South, Catholic and Presbyterian, inevitably
began to flow together, and they flowed all the more easily
because of the help Duffy and Frederick Lucas were able to
give them. Lucas was English and a Catholic convert from
Quakerism who early in 1850 transferred *The Tablet,* of
which he was the editor, to Dublin in order the better to serve

the interests of the Church and the Irish poor. Duffy, some months earlier—in September, 1849, to be exact—had restarted *The Nation* and had espoused the movement for land reform as the best means of halting the creeping destruction of the common people. He summoned a private conference of nationalists and told them that the protection of the farmers who were flying daily before the Exterminator was the most urgent business. For nationality little could be done except keep alive its traditions ; independence would only come as the end and result of previous victories. This was essentially an acceptance of O'Connell's pragmatic attitude to politics and indicated that Duffy was now thoroughly convinced of the utter impracticability of the revolutionary line that the Young Irelanders, including himself, had recently followed.

That policy had been again tried in September, 1849, in circumstances he described to Meagher. " For a few months," he wrote, " I had to meet and defeat a clamour of the Secret Society men led by Joe Brennan. They were for instant war. I had a conference with Lalor and Brennan and endeavoured to show them where they were going, but in vain. After a little they formally determined to take the field. You will gather from the newspapers an idea of the result. Only about thirty men attended the muster at Cappoquin, in your county : they attacked a police barrack led by Brennan and were put to flight in ten minutes. Brennan and a few others fled to America, four or five were transported, and the whole attempt blown to atoms. Lalor, who had been waiting at Clonmel to second the blow, was dreadfully disappointed. He immediately wrote to me that he despaired of insurrection and would join *The Nation* if I consented. He came to town immediately after and *died* before I saw him. I since have endeavoured to do justice to his memory. He was a singularly able and original man."

For as far ahead as Duffy could see, therefore, the path

to be followed was that of reform, not revolution; but
the change of front, this "rosewater" policy as it was scorn-
fully called, was anything but pleasing to the separatist
minority. The mildest of them, John Martin, as he went
into exile in June, 1849, had felt that " poor Duffy " was far
more to be pitied than any of them for he had upon him a
great and difficult responsibility. He was confident that he
would meet the difficulties of his position with unflinching
determination. But a year later, having read the files of the
new *Nation* that Duffy sent out to the prisoners in Australia, he told Mary Eva Kelly of his disappointment. Many
a time at these jovial reunions the prisoners had chanted
Duffy's lines:

> Brothers, if this day should set,
> Another yet must crown our freedom.
> *That* will come with roll of drum
> And trampling files, with *men* to lead them.

He preferred Duffy the poet to Duffy the politician who
was now saying that it was madness to talk of Ireland seizing her freedom by the strong hand. He could not believe
that Duffy intended the silly and slavish policy this implied.
" I know he would give his life for the salvation of Ireland."

Duffy had admirers as well as critics, however; among
them Carlyle, of course, and the brilliant though erratic
Wallis who had exercised so marked an influence on Thomas
Davis in his formative years. Of an early leader in the new
Nation Wallis said he had seldom read an article of which
he would have been better pleased to be the author. "When
I read Davis's dashing articles in old times I used often to
cry out ' that's my thunder', as he frequently reproduced
not only the ideas, but the illustrations and sometimes *the
identical words* that I had used in the Historical Society.
There, however, I had priority of publication, *ore rotundo,*
to plead in my favour. But you are not saying what I have

said, but anticipating what I wanted to say . . ." The paper, however, never again sold as well as it had before '48. Financial reconstructions had to be undertaken and Duffy's difficulties were not made easier when a member of his staff made away with the cash.

Duffy's approach to the land problem took two forms. He thought, first, of a new plantation of Ireland, not by strangers this time but by natives making use of the Encumbered Estates Act that had just been passed. The method was to be the establishment of a Freehold Land Society, on the model of others then appearing in England, which would buy land wholesale and resell it to smallholders. The Society was formed but lost its impetus on the resignation of Duffy from the managing committee when John Sadleir, of whom we shall hear more later, sought to have the funds placed in his own Tipperary bank and to foist upon it some properties he had already acquired. Duffy's second project was to unite with the Ulster tenantry in obtaining a reform of the Land Code. This was the idea enshrined in the Irish Tenant League which was established in August, 1850, with a Council representative of the entire country to achieve through deputations, the publication of tracts and through contested elections, the principle of fair rents fixed by valuation, fixity of tenure, and the tenant's right to dispose of his interest. These principles were conceded in an Act of 1881, but thirty years earlier they seemed to many people a startling programme, outside the reach of practical politics. They went beyond anything O'Connell considered feasible in his day, and his son John was convinced that the regulation of rents by valuation was ridiculous. The League from the start encountered opposition from the Government and from the Irish Members of Parliament, but in the country it was warmly welcomed, and county meetings held in quick succession at the instance of an organisation sub-committee of which Duffy was the chairman, drew tremendous crowds. At the first meeting at Enniscorthy, the farmers within a radius of twenty miles attended on foot and horseback and there were said to be enough burghers present to control the county election. A couple of days later eight thousand farmers, with most of the priests of the diocese of Ossory, walked into Kilkenny to hear speakers from the North and South of Ireland. It was there that Doctor McKnight in urging Irishmen of different faiths to abandon once and for all aimless distinctions of Party, grasped the hand of Father O'Shea, " an incident which roused the popular enthusiasm to a tempest ". In his turn, Father Keeffe told the gathering that they held in their hands a weapon sheathed for three hundred years, a weapon never yet tried against England, the weapon of the union of all Irishmen. The landlords' slogan was " divide and conquer "; the people of Ireland had raised the holier cry of " unite and conquer ".

From Kilkenny the League went to Ulster and there in many venues the speakers were received by processions which came with bands and ornamental banners and with messages of welcome from prominent Protestants and Catholics. Backwards and forwards the organisers travelled achieving such success that by the time the first general meeting of the League came to be held marvellous progress was reported. Hope, which had died out of the hearts of the people with the failure of the Repeal movement, had been rekindled: money, long refused for all political purposes, " came in a golden tide ". Local societies had been started in nineteen counties, laying the basis for subsequent parliamentary action; and in more than thirty constituencies members had pledged themselves to elect to Parliament only men committed to the principles of the League who could be relied upon to withhold support from any government that refused to advance those principles. Abatements of rent and even the practice of public valuation had already been voluntarily conceded by some landlords.

It was fully accepted that the real battle for the tenants would have to be fought and won in the British House of Commons, and the League wanted as far as possible to replace the sitting Irish Members of Parliament by representatives of their own. Duffy personally had little use for the existing Irish M.Ps. The few honest men among them were politically ineffective; the majority he described as habitual jobbers who were not above selling the petty appointments that were theirs to dispose of. But Duffy's comment on the situation as a whole was that a miracle had been wrought, that the unity of North and South for which Grattan and O'Connell had fought had been achieved by infinitely weaker hands. This, however, was a considerable exaggeration; the League was never more than a Southern movement with a few Northern allies, and had to face considerable opposition. McKnight and his Northern colleagues were assailed by the landlord press in Ulster; and, in the South, John O'Connell announced once a week that Duffy, who had proved such a dangerous leader in 1848, would be sure to tempt the people into illegal courses.

The League's first big test arose when following the assumption by the English Catholic Bishops of the titles of their dioceses contrary to the statute law, the Prime Minister, Lord John Russell, who had achieved office in 1846 with the help of the Irish Catholic vote, raised the " no popery " issue in his famous letter to the Anglican Bishop of Durham and in the Ecclesiastical Titles Bill, applicable to both England and Ireland, which he subsequently introduced. The enormous outburst of anti-Catholic bigotry this provoked seemed bound to affect the young Tenant League as it swung precariously on its North-South axis, while the inescapable Catholic reaction could not but be offensive to Irish Protestants.

9

At this point in the story as Duffy himself tells it in books of near-classical quality the remarkable figure of Dr. Paul Cullen appears for the first time. Duffy introduces him simultaneously with two notorious laymen, William Keogh, the Catholic Liberal member for Athlone, a brilliant political strategist whose parliamentary seat had been bought for him by a Birmingham banker, and another lawyer, John Sadleir, who since his entry into the House of Commons had become a banker and speculator and was reputed to be prodigiously rich. These two occupied the centre of the stage, while the supposed leader of the Irish Liberals in Parliament, George Henry Moore, an honest, able, but impetuous man, stood in the wings.

Cullen, formerly the Rector of the Irish College in Rome, had been appointed Archbishop of Armagh and Apostolic Delegate, but Duffy saw in him no resemblance in manners, demeanour or capacity to the great ecclesiastics who were usually sent on national missions. He was prepared to concede that he was a devoted churchman and a man of prodigious zeal and steadfastness of purpose, but " he was plain, clumsy, slow of speech, intellectually narrow and ill-informed ". His greatest defect in Duffy's eyes, however, was that he paid no regard to the character or aim of the Irish members of parliament; so long as they were fighting, as he thought, the battle of the Church, he gave them his whole sympathy while he used any influence he could command to subvert those whom he considered the enemies of the Church. Into the first category he put Sadleir and Keogh and the other Irish Liberal members whose opposition to the Ecclesiastical Titles Bill had won for them the honourable title of the Irish Brigade and who had joined in supporting a Catholic Defence Association that had been formed in Dublin. Into the second category he put Duffy and those who like him were afraid of the damage the Brigade might do to the Tenant League, in both the South and North of Ireland. Lucas, unlike Duffy, at first considered it feasible for the Catholic Defence Association to exist in parallel if not in actual alliance with the Tenant League; had they not both the idea of acting independently of the existing British political parties? Being the editor of a Catholic journal, he naturally disliked falling out with the bishops; it had indeed been the habit of his life to act with them. When the claims of the Church conflicted with secular interests he did not admit that there was any choice for him. The Church spoke to him, it was said, with the same authority from the Vatican as from Mount Sinai. Therefore, while he used his influence in private to prevent the new Catholic Defence movement from conflicting with the interests of the Tenant League, in his paper he kept in as close relation with their public action as his judgment permitted. Duffy, on the other hand, stood aloof from the Catholic Defence Association. In matters of discipline he was prepared to listen to the bishops with deference and submission, " but in politics," he said, " I must follow my own judgment and conscience, and I declined to seek counsel which I might not be able to follow ". He had no knowledge of theology or any taste for it; his ultimate concern was with getting self-government for Ireland and he was willing to apply himself to any honourable task likely to promote that end. Knowing the Irish situation better than Lucas did, he refused to recognise Sadleir and Keogh as men in whom it was safe to repose any confidence, regardless of whatever support they might pick up in the country or from the hierarchy. The wisdom of his words was to be shown in a very short time. But before that happened Cullen was to be transferred to the see of Dublin in May, 1852.

Nearly forty years later as Duffy looked back on the appointment, he recalled how it had been hoped that Propaganda would have given Dublin a worthy successor to the patriot prelate of the 12th century, Saint Laurence O'Toole, but in truth no man ever held the office who was more essentially a foreigner than Dr. Cullen. He was an Italian official, who only regarded Ireland as a convenient fulcrum for the foreign policy of the Vatican. He might have been a good bishop, Duffy thought, but assuredly he was a bad Irishman whose idea it was to transfer the government of Ireland to bishops, and to a few laymen prepared to accept their lead without question or criticism; and time had proven this policy to be a disastrous failure. But his fundamental fault, in Duffy's eyes, was that he mistook his own imperfect acquaintance with facts for profound knowledge, and acted on his prejudices as if they were inspiration. He saw the Nationalists of Ireland as a reproduction of the type of the Italian Nationalists but he failed to realise that as in Ireland the Church had been the ally and confederate of the Irish Nationalists, so the Irish Nationalists had been loyal sons of the Church. But, as a successor to Duffy in the editorial chair of *The Nation* admitted, that paper had at one time warmly written up the Carbonari, so that Cullen had a superficial reason for thinking of Duffy as an Irish Mazzini. They had met occasionally with Cullen concealing his feelings behind an affable smile, but friendly ecclesiastics warned Duffy of the truth, and his friend Lucas told him that the Archbishop had urged him to separate himself from so dangerous a connexion.

Duffy's description of the Archbishop is inaccurate in important respects. Cullen did not seek—consciously at any rate—to transfer the Government of Ireland to the bishops, or to make himself, as was said, the leader of the Irish Whigs. Neither was he in any sense a Castle bishop although that was widely alleged against him. He never attended Castle functions and refused invitations to serve on Government Commissions. He wanted to be a political neutral. In Rome and in Dublin he kept a watchful eye on every British move to obtain unfair advantage. And, as Newman put it, he was as vehement against the Young Irelanders as against the McHaleites, against the McHaleites as against the English. In this process he coldly disapproved of the appointment of Young Irelanders to the staff of the Catholic University, and may have kept Duffy out of the chair of Modern History. The belief that he did would explain a lot of Duffy's dislike of the prelate.

Cullen's involvement in politics arose out of the nature of his position and of his basic concern for Church discipline. He worked with a large measure of success to give his fellow bishops a sense of unity which they had hitherto lacked and through them to define and restrict the role of priests in political matters. This action was naturally susceptible of misinterpretation and Cullen was subsequently blamed by Duffy and others for intervening only against priests who supported the Tenant League though this was not the case. He had withheld his support from the Tenant League because Duffy's policy of Independent Opposition stood in the way, he thought, of obtaining urgently needed redress for the poor people of the country. He disliked Duffy intensely simply because he was the re-incarnation of Young Irelandism which Cullen always saw as a manifestation of continental liberalism. He also seems to have linked in his mind the Young Irelanders' concern to effect a political union of Protestants and Catholics with the proselytism that had begun with the so-called Second Reformation and that continued to be practised in the Famine years and afterwards. Protestants were not to be trusted. O'Connell, he felt, had been betrayed by every Protestant he put in a prominent position, including Davis, Mitchel and Smith O'Brien.

10

Duffy used *The Nation* in those difficult days to keep the Tenant League united and to prevent either its southern Catholic or northern Presbyterian supporters from taking undue offence in the bitter arguments that arose over the Ecclesiastical Titles Bill. For a time he appeared to be successful, for the League held together against external pressures. The tests from within its own ranks were harder to endure, however. In Limerick a League candidate was beaten into third place in a three-cornered contest for the parliamentary seat, as the result of the opposition of the local Catholic bishop. Worse still, the League's County Club in Longford put up as their candidate a landlord who was not merely a former colleague of Lord John Russell, and therefore unlikely to go into embarrassing opposition to him, but a man " who distributed . . . the employments and donations which corrupt the people and their leaders ". He was elected, so that, as Duffy put it, " one party hack was replaced by another more experienced in the arts of intrigue and corruption ". This act of treachery was denounced with scorn and indignation by *The Nation* which published the names of the priests of the Diocese of Ardagh who, to a large degree, constituted the County Club. Their bishop, Dr. Higgins, who applauded O'Connell's compact with the Whigs in 1846 and denounced the Young Irelanders as the enemies of religion, was believed to be behind the move. A priest wrote to the paper that the conduct of this club was enough to disgust and crimson with shame all Catholic men, and to tear out of the heart of Presbyterians the fibre of confidence in the Union that had been so lately cemented. And another priest declared in Belfast that he was ashamed to show himself in that city after such a foul surrender. The

people were true, he told the Northern Leaguers: the disaster
sprung from want of courage and honesty in those who
ought to be their teachers.

Another transaction even more disastrous still followed.
For Cork city, supposedly a safe seat for the popular party,
a man was returned unpledged both to the principles of the
League and to oppose the Government. In due course he
exchanged his seat " for a pleasant commissionership within
hail of Pall Mall ", for he did not care a damn for his constituents and had no hesitation in telling them so. Well
might Duffy ask that if Cork, the capital of Celtic Ireland,
the centre of the bitterest wrongs and sufferings the League
had been created to arrest, could behave like this, where
would resistance come from?

While the Tenant League was staggering under these
blows the Catholic Defence Association, supported enthus-
iastically by the majority of the English and Irish bishops,
was flourishing and Keogh, its leader, had a signal success
when he induced Sharman Crawford to join forces with him
in presenting a Land Bill to Parliament. Duffy was appalled
that an honest, intelligent man like Crawford could make a
mistake that imposed a gang of shameless jobbers on the
people and set back for a whole generation the principles
he represented. But Crawford's defence was that the League
had not at that time a single representative in the House
of Commons. He wanted to get something done, and turned
away from " a bunch of agitators " to the Irish Brigade,
which he could see had the solid backing of eminent
churchmen.

Other moves of the Catholic Defence Association were to
start in 1852 a newspaper of its own, the *Catholic Telegraph*
in opposition to the *Tablet* and at half the price, and to
exclude other newspaper proprietors and editors from their
ranks. This was aimed at Lucas, who from being a supporter
of theirs had lost confidence in them and had begun to scoff

at their affectation of patriotism. Duffy warned in *The Nation*
against any gagging of the press and when one of the
Oxford converts, Henry Wilberforce, was appointed secretary of the Association, he cautioned the Irish people
against the denationalising process of introducing Englishmen
and Anglo-Irishmen into positions of power and influence.
This had been demonstrated by the election in Limerick of
Lord Arundel and by the fact that " several English candidates were notoriously negotiating for Irish constituencies ". Archbishop Cullen, however, thought it reasonable and proper that Wilberforce should be appointed because
the Catholic Defence Association was a United Kingdom
affair. Archbishop McHale of Tuam thought differently;
and a compromise was achieved by giving Wilberforce an
Irish assistant.

When, following the defeat of Lord John Russell on a
militia bill and a short period of office for the Tories under
Lord Derby, the general election did eventually occur in
1852, the Irish Tenant League was not in particularly good
trim. Funds were low, and the leaders were embarrassed
by " wealthy nincompoops " who were only interested in
the League as a stepping stone into Parliament. It was far
from easy to find in a poor country like Ireland fifty or sixty
candidates with the necessary property qualification who
could afford to live in London for six months of the year at
their own expense and who could be relied upon to support
an unpopular course; but the Council of the League made
the attempt and Duffy in *The Nation* explained the policy
by which alone he believed the cause might be carried to
success, the policy of Independent Opposition. In the parliamentary struggle Ireland held the key to the position. She
was ready to say to the opposing groups—" debate and
divide, gentlemen, it is your right; but Ireland must decide
who shall have the majority ". This was the talismanic
sentence which would open the ears of the English parties

to the Irish question. Whatever party could obtain control of the House of Commons would rule the Empire. Fifty disciplined Irishmen of integrity and capacity could overturn any ministry simply by walking across the floor of the House.

The Catholic Defence Association had their own ideas about candidates for the election. They knew, for instance, whom they did not want. Lucas was one such person, and when he was suggested by the Leaguers for Meath they endeavoured, with the support of the bishop, to keep him from getting a nomination. However, the priests and the people of Meath resisted this move and passed a resolution declaring that some of the Catholic Defence Association people who had been pushing candidates on Irish constituencies were exterminating landlords whose guidance was not to be trusted. Duffy hailed Lucas' nomination; he would be an incomparable Leaguer and a whole Catholic Defence Association in himself. His impregnable coolness and masculine vigour, his resources, and the reserve of vehement passion which great occasions call out, would make him a master of that practical eloquence which sways the House of Commons. In due course, Lucas was elected with a majority of four to one.

11

Duffy was one of three candidates proposed by the Council of the League for consideration by the local election committee in New Ross. He was advised to present himself to the constituency in the company of Father Tom O'Shea, one of the famous Callan curates, but on reaching Callan he found Father O'Shea sick with bronchitis. Despite his condition and the broken weather, Father O'Shea insisted on travelling to New Ross, and he did so, in an open car, muffled to the chin. He also made the preliminary call on Father Doyle, the senior curate in the town, who had been a fellow-student of his in former days and who was understood to exercise a decisive influence over the election committee who were mostly Old Irelanders. Father Doyle was a hard nut to crack: he had nothing against Duffy personally but he would not agree to propose him. Later, however, when he talked things over with Duffy and Father O'Shea together, he consented to let the candidate be interviewed and next morning eighteen or twenty members of the committee assembled for that purpose and were joined by Father Doyle who, wrapped up in a heavy cloak and muffler because of influenza, told them that he had come to look on but would take no part in the proceedings. There were other passing onlookers—three or four members of the committee came to the door and stared in for a minute or two as at some strange animal, and then took their departure. " I had formed a resolution during a sleepless night to make that day a cardinal one in my life," Duffy wrote later; " it might be one of discomfiture and disaster; but at any rate it should be signal and decisive. I told the committee I had been forewarned of their prejudice against me because I was associated with men whom I believed to be the most enlightened and disinterested whom Ireland had known in this century, but they had probably only heard one side of the case, and should now hear the other. A committee, who were all Irishmen, were probably all repealers, and who had the additional bond of sympathy that they were all Catholic, afforded as fair a tribunal as I could ever hope to appeal to on my past career and my present designs, and I had come to the fixed resolution of accepting their verdict as final, whatever it might be. If after hearing my defence of the conduct of the Young Irelanders, and my aims in entering Parliament, they declared that I was not a fit candidate for New Ross, I would abandon my candidature, resign my seat on the Council of the League, discontinue *The Nation,* and retire from Irish affairs for ever. This was my fixed determination, and I spoke for an hour under the strong feeling created by the belief that it was my last appeal to an Irish audience.

I do not know, and I can never know, to what extent I won the sympathy of the committee, for a factor came into play which baffled all calculations. As soon as I sat down Father Doyle stripped off his cloak and muffler, and plunged into the business. He declared he would give me his unequivocal support, and made a passionate appeal for fair play, before which opposition seemed gradually to melt away. There were thrilling cheers, as he urged point after point, which were not for the orator solely, and when I withdrew I believed that a majority of the committee were prepared to support me."

Duffy got the nomination and found himself opposed in the election by Sir Thomas Redington, the former Under Secretary for Ireland, and Henry Lambert who had represented the County Wexford twenty years earlier. He was supported most valiantly by Father Doyle, notwithstanding the opposition of his Parish Priest who preferred Redington

as a Catholic gentleman who had served his country with
distinction. As for Duffy, he told a congregation in the presence of Duffy himself that Duffy was aiming at a position
which neither God nor man had intended for him or him
for. The landlord of the town also warned his tenants against
having anything to do with a man who was the enemy of the
rights of property.

Duffy considered himself fortunate in his antagonists.
Lambert had been elected as a Repealer in 1832 but had
deserted O'Connell in the House of Commons and was
known to the people as Luttrell Lambert. The significance
of the " Luttrell " hardly needed to be underlined to make
its impact on the voters. He was able to flay Redington for
having as a minister in Russell's Government armed the
Orangemen against the Repealers in 1848, packed juries
against political prisoners by excluding Catholics, suborned
Birch and Conway to malign the Young Irelanders and
helped to pass the Ecclesiastical Titles Act, while as a landlord he had expelled a hundred and eighty persons from his
Galway property since the Famine. Redington canvassed
the borough preceded by a troop of dragoons, a company
of infantry and three detachments of police and followed by
a hired retinue of disreputable tenants, but neither the display
of pomp nor the use of intimidation and bribery had much
influence on the electors. Interest in such an election could
not be confined to the constituency. It was a topic of conversation everywhere and the newspapers were full of it.
The Reform Club in London was reported to be putting up
money to secure Duffy's defeat and this rumour led to the
opening of a fund for Duffy which was so successful that the
election did not cost him a shilling piece. Money came from
America through the efforts of John Dillon and Richard
O'Gorman while many of Duffy's friends in England contributed generously. Among the Irish subscribers were
Father Theobald Mathew the temperance reformer, and

Doctor T. W. Croke, who had already begun to accumulate the prestige that was later associated with his occupancy of the See of Cashel. Duffy's name, he wrote, fell like a house-hold word upon Irish ears; his repute became greater as he himself grew more mature; and the heroic devotion to the cause of nationality of which he had already given the most unequivocal proofs was his best security for future services.

In the upshot, Duffy won a resounding victory. Redington withdrew from the contest, and left Lambert, aided by the town landlord and a small Tory following, to face the bulk of the electors who, marshalled and disciplined by Father Doyle, stayed together overnight to await the opening of the polling booths. Among them were Duffy's bitterest Old Ireland opponents in the election committee. By noon the contest was over and Duffy had a majority of more than two to one. In the blaze of enthusiasm that followed, he realised that his victory was due to the young priests headed by Father Doyle and to the leadership they had given the people. Had there been time in 1848 to overcome the mass of prejudice against the Young Irelanders, a similar result could, he thought, have been achieved on a national scale.

12

The result of the General Election and of conferences held subsequently was that nearly fifty Irish Liberals went to Westminster, on the reassembly in November, 1852, committed to the principle of independent opposition. This number included, of course, the Catholic Defence Association brigadiers who had made common cause with the Tenant Leaguers. They entered Parliament effectively holding the balance of power provided they acted together, voting for every measure of benefit to Ireland and rejecting those that were harmful to Irish interests.

It was not long before there was a change of Government. Disraeli, who was Lord Derby's Chancellor of the Exchequer, introduced his first budget and this the Irish Party might have supported had not Derby made it known that under no circumstances would his Government accept the principles of Sharman Crawford's Bill which the Irish had sponsored. The Tories were defeated by a majority of nineteen and were replaced by a combination of Whigs and Peelites under Lord Aberdeen. It was at this point that the so-called Independent Opposition suffered a blow from which it never recovered. On the publication of the lists of junior ministers it was found that Sadleir had been appointed a Lord of the Treasury and Keogh Irish Solicitor General and other appointments from the ranks of the Irish were forecasted. For the moment, however, attention was focussed upon Sadleir and Keogh because these men had pledged themselves in the most deliberate fashion never to support, much less to take office from, a Government not pledged to repeal the Ecclesiastical Titles Bill, to abolish the Church

Establishment, and to deal with the land problem on the lines adumbrated by Sharman Crawford. And here was a Government to whom these things were plainly impossible. A storm of protest rose against the deserters. They were denounced in the national press and from public platforms. G. H. Moore who had hitherto supported Keogh accused him of a breach of morality, and five bishops headed by McHale cast him off. It seemed an unmitigated disaster, and yet the loss of numbers was offset by a temporary gain in spirit for those who remained loyal to their pledges. These men drew closer together. Trouble, however, arose in another quarter. It had been noted that Archbishop Cullen had remained silent when Sadleir and Keogh defected. Now Duffy saw him at the head of a conspiracy of bishops. " We failed at that time and place ", he declared, " because we were betrayed by prelates in whom the people had a blind confidence ".

Duffy found the incessant parliamentary round and the demands of the Irish clients exhausting. Yet he had to work simultaneously at his profession as a journalist. He was *The Nation's* parliamentary correspondent as well as its editor and this imposed upon him the heavy task of supplying the paper regularly with an elaborate comment on the proceedings of the House in the manner of the period. But it was not the burden of work only that affected him but the presence in the House, alongside the Tory agents of Irish landlords and a Whig majority that scoffed at Irish claims, of the group of Irish deserters who had been elected by the suffrage of a suffering people. These men, he kept on emphasising, were supported by the majority of the Irish bishops, so that, as time went on, " whenever a candidate went to the hustings in the name of the Independent Opposition his fate was to be hamstrung from behind by the crozier of some Whig Prelate ". Yet Duffy, and Lucas who shared these feelings with him, fought off the enveloping despair,

and in *The Nation* and *The Tablet* they told their readers
to have patience because success in the English Parliament
was a notoriously slow process.

But things got worse instead of better. The Ulster Tenant
Right party sided with the deserters in the Select Committee
that examined Crawford's Bill and Crawford advised the
tenant farmers to accept a measure more modest than his
own. What upset the League leaders most, however, was
his implied belief that the two men who had accepted office
had not violated their pledges but had put themselves in a
position to advance the tenants' case. From there he proceeded to disparage and misrepresent the policy of the
Independent Opposition and to move into a position of
general antipathy in which he was joined by, of all people,
Doctor McKnight. When by-elections occurred, as they inevitably did, the League candidates were beaten by a combination of Government supporters, landlords, bishops and a
majority of the local clergy. " There was always," Duffy
wrote, " a group of patriotic priests in a constituency ready
to face all consequences; but the world, the flesh and the
devil were often too strong for them." As for the people,
they had many excuses for lethargy, but what, he asked,
can you do for people who will do nothing for themselves?

Corruption was so universally triumphant that national
feeling became almost afraid to show itself; and Duffy cited
three cases to justify this condemnation. O'Connell's
youngest son had resigned his seat in order it was said to
accept a consulship, and the arrangement having fallen
through he was helped by the clergy into another seat in
Tralee from which he lent the Government support whenever they needed it. In the course of his election a furious
mob howled down the League candidate for daring to
oppose the son of the Liberator. In Clare two expert jobbers
who had uniformly supported the Government and who had
been unseated for intimidation were re-elected, it being

alleged that their opponent was an exterminator; but, as Duffy pointed out, their re-election pulled down more roof trees in the future than Colonel Vandeleur had done in the past. In the third case a bigoted Protestant candidate was deliberately imported into the constituency from England in order to create an atmosphere in favour of the election of John Sadleir as the champion of Catholic interests.

The Leaguers tried to save the policy of Independent Opposition by holding another conference of their supporters. This was sparsely attended, and it was apparent from the outset that the delegates were divided on the correctness or otherwise of Sadleir and Keogh's behaviour. Charges were followed by countercharges and while a vote of confidence in the Independent Party and of censure on the deserters was ultimately adopted, it had the effect of driving the men from the North out of the Conference. Dr. McKnight charged Lucas with treachery to the cause in that he had privately advised the Chief Secretary for Ireland to lay aside his land proposals and postpone legislation. Lucas denied this allegation emphatically, but his word was not accepted. After the conference, Crawford, in a letter written for publication, stated that he would do no further business with him except in the presence of witnesses; this was the only way, he held, to deal with a person so given to misstatement and equivocation. The Northerners had always feared Lucas as an incurable bigot and from the foundation of the League Dr. McKnight took as much pains to warn Duffy against Lucas as Dr. Cullen had earlier taken to warn Lucas against Duffy. Duffy was convinced that Crawford was misled into being grossly unjust to Lucas while Lucas, in the height of his indignation, used language which a cold, proud man like Crawford could never forgive. He had unfortunately the knack of turning timid friends into active enemies. The League finally had to make a choice and Duffy made the choice for it by taking sides against his old Northern allies and with Lucas who, he said, was the man of the highest integrity and plainest disinterestedness he knew.

This Lucas/Duffy combination did not last long: it was shattered in an affair with the bishops which began with the removal to an inferior rural parish of Duffy's friend and ally, Father Doyle. Father Doyle should not have been surprised by this treatment for at the general election he had carried his zeal for Duffy to the point of publicly insulting his parish priest who supported another candidate. Father O'Shea of Callan renown was recalled and narrowly escaped suspension for campaigning miles and miles away from his parish and diocese. In his case also the exercise of discipline was not out of place. Nevertheless in both instances Duffy and Lucas and Company were left with a feeling of uneasiness in their minds; and a third case involving Father Keeffe, the other Callan curate, convinced them that a campaign was being waged against them from within the ecclesiastical Province of Dublin. In a private letter Father Keeffe had reproached the local member Sergeant Shee for abandoning his colleagues on some matter of parliamentary tactics, and Shee retaliated by publishing the letter with his reply, whereupon the Bishop of Ossory forbade Father Keeffe from taking any further part in politics, as he had done in the case of Fr. O'Shea. The bishop's act seemed thoroughly arbitrary; if it became a precedent no priest who supported the policy of Independent Opposition could be safe in giving his aid to the party; and so, following a public demonstration in Callan, an appeal was taken by Lucas to Rome on behalf of the members of parliament in which all their grievances were raised, including recent synodal statutes which limited the political activity of the clergy. Other appeals from the priests directly concerned and from others were nipped in the bud by ecclesiastical action.

Lucas, despite ill-health, diligently prosecuted what has been described as an unnecessary appeal to Rome; unnecessary because of the League's misinterpretation of Cullen's policy for which Cullen, who was indifferent to public relations, was largely to blame. The Pope in private audiences appeared sympathetic and suggested a conference with Cullen who was in Rome for the Vatican Council. This, when held, proved a disaster. In the course of it Cullen broke into a violent tirade against Duffy whom he described as a wicked man, to act with whom after his conduct in 1848 was impossible until he had fasted fifty years on bread and water. Lucas defended Duffy and mentioned the evidence of Bishops Blake and Moriarty at his trial. Moriarty had testified that from his acquaintance he had considered Duffy as a man of the highest and purest principles of integrity and honour, a peace-loving man and an enemy of anarchy. He also knew him to be a professing and believing and practical Christian. At this the Cardinal became more violent. Duffy, he said, had been a party to getting the people massacred ; ridiculed the notion of his being a pious man, declared that he did not care what the Bishops had sworn ; and then turning upon Lucas, said it was discreditable for him to say a word on behalf of such a man, or to act with him. The particular cause of this passionate outburst was some articles in *The Nation* which Duffy admitted were powerfully plain and direct but neither rude nor disrespectful. In one of these Duffy said that if some of the best priests in Ireland had been sent to rot in bogs and morasses, if a bishop of the Church of God had mounted a platform with a man of the character of William Keogh, if political profligacy had lost much of its horror in the eyes of the people, the chief cause was the alliance between the Archbishop of Dublin and the Catholic agents of Dublin Castle. The fear of the Apostolic Delegate weighed like lead on the Irish priesthood, and rendered all public action driftless and impotent. That statement was untrue in its most important point, for, as we said earlier, far from being in cahoots with

Dublin Castle, Cullen kept away from it altogether ; his sole visit, so far as we know, took place years after this and its purpose was to obtain a reprieve for a Fenian condemned to death.

When Duffy met Lucas he hardly recognised him, so terribly had he wilted under the strain of his Roman mission which Duffy conceived had failed although the Pope had not yet pronounced on Lucas's memorial. Duffy came to the conclusion that Lucas and he should both retire and that the Tenant League should be dissolved; only by such action would the Irish people recognise the authors of the calamity that had befallen their cause. Lucas did not agree nor did he accept Duffy's description of the state of Irish politics. Bishop Moriarty likewise tried to dissuade Duffy, but Dr. Croke shared Duffy's view that all hope in Irish affairs was dead and buried, justifying Duffy's phrase that till a full change occurred there seemed to be no more hope for the Irish cause than for the corpse on the dissecting table. He told his constituents in a farewell address that the Irish Party was reduced to a handful, the popular organisation had been deserted by those who created it, prelates of the Irish Church thronged the ranks of their opponents, priest was arraigned against priest, and parish against parish, shameless political profligacy was openly defended and applauded, the special opportunity sent by Heaven for their deliverance was bartered away to an English faction, and the ultimate aim for which he had laboured, to give back to Ireland her national existence, was forgotten or disdained.

In the upshot Duffy alone resigned, Lucas died soon after and his paper passed into Whig hands, Moore lost his seat in the next general election, and the League gradually dissolved. Duffy's subsequent career in the House of Commons has been described by the Irish historian, J. H. Whyte, as rather a disappointment, that during those three years he was less influential than at any other period in his career, and that his speeches made little impact. However, in 1853 he made a stand against the Government for practising corruption on Irish members and was called to account; and at the instance of the Irish in Sydney and Melbourne he was benevolently active when the Constitution framed by the Australian colonies came to Westminster for confirmation. In the 1854 session he did not speak at all because of ill-health. Nonetheless he was a significant figure in the House and he was understandably impressed by some of the men he met there—Bright and Cobden in particular. Disraeli he got to know, too, and admired the ability of this English Jew to overcome the difficulties in his path. Gladstone was "smooth as silk", and Duffy noted how the vigour and grace of his rhetoric put criticism to flight. As for Palmerston, Duffy seemed to accept Carlyle's judgment that he was a fitting leader for an age without sincerity or veracity.

13

While still a member Duffy was involved in another controversy which was to be prolonged and bitter. His antagonist was John Mitchel who, on surrendering his parole in a manner that Duffy considered utterly reprehensible, had escaped from Australia, and gone to New York where he began to publish his *Jail Journal*, including comments on the news that reached him from Ireland. In this series, which he later brought out in book form, he accused Duffy of having encouraged " poor O'Brien upon his Tipperary war " of which he was particularly contemptuous, and of producing evidence in defence of his " fine private character " and hinted that, in order to relieve the enemy from all embarrassment in their vindication of the law, he had allowed a craven petition for mercy to be extensively signed on his behalf and presented to the Government. Sarcastically he denied being angry with Duffy who could not be expected " to get himself hulked for any principle, object, or cause whatsoever "; and alleged that when Duffy was released from prison and announced his intention of restarting *The Nation*, he had urged the Government to put no obstacle in his way, for the paper would, for the future, be perfectly constitutional, safe and legal. His final insult was to call him Mr. Give-in Duffy, the candidate for New Ross. Duffy was naturally outraged by all this. Even if the accusations were partly true, he would have been angry, but they were not for, as Arthur Griffith pointed out, the articles in *The Nation* which were supposed to have sent O'Brien out on his Tipperary War were not written by Duffy at all, while in calling evidence as to his private character he was following precedent, and was warranted, in any event, in doing so because the Government and the Government press were systematically trying to blacken the character of the Young Irelanders in order to excite public feeling against them. And what Mitchel did not know was that Duffy had rejected a Government offer to release him if he would plead guilty formally.

Duffy answered Mitchel along these lines in correspondence in *The Nation*. He also counter-attacked. Mitchel, he said, was a recklessly violent man, who had pluck and rhetorical power but no commonsense. He owed his position and his opportunities to Duffy. He had misunderstood and presumed on Duffy's silence in '48 and subsequently. In 1848 Duffy had kept silent because conflict between them at that time would have torn the Confederation to shreds and since '48 Duffy would not speak so long as Mitchel was in prison. "It is not in your nature," he told Mitchel, "to comprehend a forbearance which postponed personal feelings in public policy—you, who prepared for an insurrection in '48 by outraging half the insurgents, and who smoothed the way for your invasion of Ireland in '54 by libelling every public movement and public man in the country." Duffy denied that he had sent O'Brien to Ballingarry but, while he felt under no obligation to defend the failure of the insurrection that was attempted, he would not have it disparaged by Mitchel whose theory of revolution, he said, was reducible to two maxims worthy of bedlam—namely that whatever was meditated against the English Government should be proclaimed beforehand, and that officers or preparations were superfluous. When Mitchel was arrested, he had not a barrel of gunpowder or a case of muskets. His resources literally began and ended in a bag of wind.

He accused Mitchel of having stolen Lalor's ideas, of calling them his own, of having that claim believed by people, and of hating everybody, but chiefly Duffy, who was acquainted with the imposture. He alleged that Lalor was

so enraged at what had been done to him that he retired
from the movement until after Mitchel's transportation. " Do
you really believe," Duffy asked him, " that you have
bequeathed anything to Ireland which gives you the right to
be our censor? Your opinions are a fragment of Davis's
which you misunderstood, and a bundle of Lalor's which
you have appropriated. In your career there is but one
moment that can be recalled with unmixed satisfaction—
your attitude in the dock. It might have saved your name;
but with that blind impatience which was ever your bane,
you have forfeited it. You have blotted it out of the memory
of men by the disgraceful breach of your parole. You have
made, as far as in you lies, the word of an Irish gentleman
of less value in the universe. You have prepared for future
political prisoners utter distrust of their pledges. Do not
presume, sir, to palter with the facts. A moment spent in
a police office, where careful precautions were taken beforehand by money and diplomacy, to make the proceeding a
farce, was not a release from your parole. It is not so a
gentleman fulfils his obligations; he is careful to be rather
in excess than in deficiency in matters of honour."

Duffy maintained this position until the end of his days.
But O'Brien thought that two opinions could reasonably
be entertained regarding the parole. " For myself," he told
Duffy, " I always endeavour if possible to justify my friends
when there is a doubt about their conduct, nay even when
they are wrong. But in this case I really consider that Mitchel
was not bound to anything more than the strict letter of the
engagement. No confidence was placed in us. We were not
treated as gentlemen. Our parole was extorted not in order
to confer advantage upon us but as a *security* to the Government. I regret, however, not that you should have thought
Mitchel's escape incompatible with his parole—but that you
should have thought it necessary in vindication of yourself to
fling this charge upon him. I know that his friends, parti-

cularly John Martin and P. J. Smyth, both of whom I honour as amongst the most truly chivalrous men that I have ever known, were deeply hurt on finding that such an accusation came from *you*. Let us say no more however upon this point as it is a sore one to all parties."

14

Duffy made up his mind to quit the "blind and bitter land" of Ireland and gave as his reason for doing so that an Ireland where Mr. Keogh typified patriotism and Dr. Cullen the Church was an Ireland he could not live in. But this, though one reason for his going, was not the only one. He had an abiding sense of personal failure, for all the movements with which he was associated had come to nothing. His health, moreover, was wretched; overwork and anxiety had frequently brought him to the point of danger ; and he could hardly forget that he was the only surviving member of his family, and that his doctor had told him he had only one lung. "I have laboured until my health broke down," he told Smith O'Brien who at the end of 1854 was still a prisoner in Van Diemen's Land. "I have neglected my family and lived only for the Irish cause and at every point I have found myself thwarted by men who thought themselves justified in abusing me for my share in the affairs of '48—landlords, bishops and Government officials—or for resisting O'Connell. After twelve years of fruitless struggle my heart is weary and longs for tranquillity . . ."

He thought of Australia, a country that had been much in his mind because of the part he was called upon to play in connexion with the confirmation of the Constitutions of the Colonies. He was sure the climate would be beneficial to his health and from his consultations with distinguished Australians he believed that in Victoria particularly there would be opportunities for becoming a successful lawyer and living a contented social life. He had naturally much to do before he could leave ; but his principal concern was with the future of Smith O'Brien and of Maynooth College. He campaigned among supporters of the Government and the Opposition for permission for O'Brien to return to Ireland and spent a few days with him in Brussels before he left for Australia. He also used whatever influence he had with the Parliamentary Select Committee that had been appointed to investigate the affairs of Maynooth on behalf of his friends in the College who feared a move by Dr. Cullen to obtain personal control over the institution in order " to denationalise it, to Italianise it, and crush the professors who cherished some spirit of independence." He had then to dispose of his interest in *The Nation* which he did to A. M. Sullivan and Michael Clery, arranging that they were to retain Cashel Hoey as editor, who had been his own part proprietor and associate editor from the revival of the paper in 1849. With the help of a loan from Thomas O'Hagan he cleared the debts that had arisen as a result of his public career. He had always insisted on paying his way, and could honestly say that he had never accepted so much as a postage stamp by way of reward or compensation for his public service.

In October, 1855, he sailed on the " Ocean Chief " with his wife and three of his children, and with only £20 in his pocket. John, his eldest boy, had gone to Stonyhurst to be educated at grandfather McLaughlin's expense. The emotional strain was oppressive as Duffy considered the step he had taken, to leave Ireland for a country on the other side of the world where he knew next to no one. " My ribs seemed to close on my heart with a painful and perilous responsibility," he wrote ; " but my wife bade me trust in God, and we faced the future without trepidation." On his first Sunday at sea he read prayers for the hundred-odd Irish Catholic emigrants among the passengers. In that year, 1855, sixteen thousand Irish went to Australia, or roughly twenty per cent of the total emigration from Ireland. In

1856 the emigrants included Duffy's highly talented cousin Margaret Hughes, Mrs. Callan, who travelled out with her doctor husband and some of her five children. One of these, another Margaret, subsequently married Duffy's eldest son, John. Mrs. Callan brought with her to Australia a rich family tradition which she had barely begun to record when she died in Melbourne in the mid-eighteen-sixties. Her great-grandfather had a store house of legends which he used recount in verse at wakes and quiltings and when the men gathered round the spinning-wheels of their women-folk during the long winter evenings. Her grandfather played the flute and taught her to sing, and often set her dancing to her shadow while he played or lilted a lively tune. At other times he would tell her stories from the *Arabian Nights,* or read to her from his large Douai Bible which she brought to Australia with her. Her father was a flax buyer when at twenty-three he married Susan Gavan, then eighteen years old, who was the sister of Duffy's mother, Anne. He was an independent-minded man who once walked the seventy miles from Dublin to Newry rather than ask his relatives for the fare. Australia was certainly enriched by some grafts from this stock.

Duffy's arrival in Victoria early in 1856 roughly coincided with the sensational news from Ireland that John Sadleir, having speculated and lost the vast sums of money entrusted to him, had committed suicide. Melbourne was no more than a thriving village, but in it he received a hero's welcome from an enormous crowd of Irishmen who came to meet him, led by John O'Shanassy who was known to his enemies as the Irish papist demagogue draper.

A public dinner was given in his honour at which he made a statement he was never allowed to hear the end of. Having proclaimed Australia as a land where there was fair play for all, he declared that in such a land he could be what nature intended him to be, if national injustice and fraud had not turned his blood into gall, a man who lent a willing and cheerful obedience to the laws and who desired no more than to be permitted to live in peace under their protection. " But let me not be misunderstood," he added, " I am not here to repudiate or apologise for any part of my past life. I am still an Irish rebel to the backbone and spinal marrow. A rebel for the same reason that John Hampden and Algernon Sydney, and George Washington and Charles Carroll of Carrolltown were rebels—because tyranny has supplanted law in my native country. I would not be tempted by all the gold in Australia to repudiate my share in a struggle which was as just and holy a one as ever was lost or won in this world. But having been a good Irishman in my old home would not, I conceived, be a bad security for my becoming a good Australian in my new one." He was a radical reformer so far as the principles of public liberty were concerned, but he was no more a Red Republican, as someone had alleged, he said, than a Red Indian.

Although tempted to settle in Sydney which he found on a visit to be about a hundred years ahead of Melbourne and where there was a much larger Irish population, Duffy preferred Melbourne where he had been so graciously received and where from the outset some legal business had come his way. Here, too, despite his original intentions to shun politics, he allowed himself to be drawn by his friends into active State affairs. " There was a work to be done," he wrote, " to gratify the highest patriotism or ambition, for here was to be laid the corner stone and foundation of a new empire." Picking up a silly sentiment that was rather common at the time he declared that some day Australia would claim as its inheritance the thousand teeming islands of the Pacific which would carry Christian civilisation into the swarming hives of China; and in the fulness of time would grasp the sceptre of India. It may also have been an exaggeration for him to say that if he had chosen to traffic in situations he could have come out to Victoria as its governor; but we do not share a view recently expressed that this statement could have had no vestige of truth or that it necessarily demonstrated the "fatal vanity" of the man. It can, however, be seen that it played into the hands of those who did not relish his arrival among them and gave them something to laugh at. "He fancies himself a whale among minnows", one of them wrote.

He had arrived at a turning point in the history of the colony, when parliamentary government was replacing government from London. The first parliament sat from 1856 to 1861 and in those five years there were to be six ministries and a bewildering assortment of factions and shuffling alliances. Duffy found his starting point in this medley without any difficulty. He was nominated for a constituency by the rising popular party which was largely Irish and which purchased for him a residence and other property in order to provide him with the qualifications required by the constitution, and was elected following a campaign conducted on lines familiar to him at home.

He found everywhere an eager curiosity about Ireland, and a knowledge of the character and characteristics of its leaders that astonished him. He was experiencing peace of mind for the first time for many years, and already had a feeling of achievement. Only for the absence of a few friends he would have been very happy indeed. "If you were not encumbered with an estate," he told G. H. Moore, "I would strive to seduce you here. What a career you would have! We are making a newer and better America. All is growth and progress and a sense of life that imparts itself to all who are handling public affairs. The seed is sown and grown and reaped in a span. You propose work and it is done. You expose an abuse and it is abandoned. I am not idealising but reporting nakedly my experience." But he told the novelist Carleton that while he never for a moment regretted having left Ireland where John Keogh and Archbishop Cullen predominated, there was no country like the old country, and no friends like the old friends. "The slopes of Howth, the hills of Wicklow and the friends of manhood are things not to be matched in this golden land." A letter he had had from Moore made him ask again if there was any hope—the faintest glimpse on the remotest point of the horizon—for Ireland. Since he had left, Monsignor Barnabo had written from Rome forbidding some Meath priests from attending meetings of the Tenant League without Dr. Cullen's express permission. Duffy exploded when he heard of this. "If the country bears in silence that most scandalous aggression of Barnabo's on the Meath priests, I will not believe there is any hope," he told Moore. "The Lord God be thanked I am living among Irish Catholics who would go to the stake rather than deny their faith, but who would fling that insolent missive into the Yarra Yarra. It makes my blood boil to think of a peasant in a mitre, a shallow, conceited dogmatist, a dense mass of prejudice and ignorance, squatting down upon the Irish cause and smothering it. What is the use, my friend, of motions in Parliament and meetings in Dublin if this stupid tyranny is to remain triumphant and unquestioned?"

He was a most constructive member of parliament, introducing or supporting proposals for abolishing property qualifications, for the federation of the colonies, for reforming the procedural methods of the new parliament in accordance with his British House of Commons experience, and securing the replacement of the special oath that Catholics only were required to take by an oath of allegiance common to all legislators and office-holders. When the government was defeated and O'Shanassy was asked by the Governor to form an administration pending an election, he did so in consultation with Duffy whom he appointed Minister for Public Works and Commissioner of Roads and Buildings.

By this time Duffy's reluctance to re-engage in politics had completely evaporated, and he was obsessed by the need to demonstrate that the Irish could succeed in Australia where they had failed in Ireland. But while Duffy insisted that the Irish were quite fitted to bear the burden of a State, his political opponents declared otherwise. They recalled Ireland's political and religious background which had made Duffy not merely an Irish rebel hostile to all peaceful government but a bitter Papist that would never be content until the Pope was proclaimed sovereign of the Australians. This was a particularly laughable suggestion to make about a man who, as he pointed out to Bishop Moriarty of Kerry, had been howled down at one end of the earth for betraying the interests of religion, and at the other end for being its slave and missionary.

O'Shanassy's first ministry lasted only three months but he was back again in office after a short interval with Duffy as President of the Board of Land and Works. In the government Duffy found himself in a minority—" there was apparently," he said, " a jealousy of the individual position I occupied in public life as a man of certain experience and knowledge," but he admitted that part of the trouble was that he was sometimes too peremptory and brusque in controversy. O'Shanassy and he began to pull apart and on the issue of the reservation of alluvial land for the people and the system of deferred payments for the purchase of land, Duffy ultimately resigned, but not before he had suffered an illness so severe that his death was actually announced in Parliament. At the following general election the Irish among the electors stood by Duffy notwithstanding his break with the popular O'Shanassy whose government was defeated at the polls. In the new parliament O'Shanassy's group occupied a corner only of the opposition front bench and became known as the Corner Party to distinguish them from the main opposition which gathered around Duffy and made him their leader in recognition of the reputation he had brought to Australia as a political organiser.

The differences between O'Shanassy and Duffy were never healed. They were deep and bitter and recreated on Australian soil the Irish alignments and feuds of the previous decade. It was not merely the confrontation of a blunt and honest man with an educated and rather class-conscious gentleman ; " O'Shanassy was essentially the *Catholic* and Duffy the *Irish* spokesman ". O'Shanassy was an O'Connellite who had migrated before the rise of the Young Ireland party and was hardly touched by the liberal influences of the day. He once claimed that control of education by the Church was an essential dogma; Duffy argued that it was, rather, a practice and a policy. He himself had been educated at a Presbyterian school where he was the only Catholic boy, and he should be sorry to think, he said, that he had violated any dogma of his faith. Irish Catholic emigrants tended to take sides for one or other of the two men and scandalous stories were put into circulation, among them that Duffy had been an informer in 1848. This O'Shanassy apparently believed till his dying day.

Duffy's new position at the head of an opposition group appealed to him. It gave him an opportunity of organising and training them for government. In Ireland opposition had meant pulling down the existing order; here there was an opportunity of employing whatever was best in the habits and institutions of free countries to build up the new state of Victoria. So far as policy was concerned, his aim, as might have been expected, was to hold a middle road position between the working classes and the land monopolists. In the following general election the government was badly beaten and the problem arose of finding an alternative ministry among the disparate opposition parties. Dr. Quinn, the Catholic Bishop of Brisbane, who had been a solid friend of Duffy's, brought him and O'Shanassy together in an uneasy truce so that together with William C. Haines, William Nicholson and J. G. Francis they were able to give the colony a strong, experienced and able administration. Duffy was once more in charge of the Land Department and introduced a comprehensive measure, known as the Duffy Land Act, the main object of which was to make the possession of land as nearly universal as possible. He had particularly in mind to give the large class of diggers something to turn to when they became unfit for the search after gold; otherwise he feared that their discontent would endanger the public safety. He also hoped to see a multitude of his own countrymen, who had been driven from the land in Ireland, find prosperity on the genial soil of Victoria. This government was defeated in 1865 on an amending Land Bill and was replaced by one under James McCulloch that with two short interruptions lasted seven years.

15

Duffy availed of the opportunity of being out of office to make a visit home with his wife and eldest daughter; he needed a holiday, for his none too robust physique had suffered from the strain of his political activities. The climate of Australia suited him well and he had a beautiful garden in which he liked to potter; but late nights, angry personal altercations, and too anxious an interest in party politics had left their mark on him. In Ireland, he told himself in his diary, he had a cause for which he was willing and was bound "to spend and be spent" without stint, but there was no such duty in Australia. He still ambitioned to hold office again "and the highest office for a time" but he did not desire to remain permanently on the battlefield of party politics with their sudden fluctuations, merciless slanders and engrossing anxieties. At the same time he recognised that he was never less happy than in 1843 when he had an ample income but was discontented with his intellectual progress. So, as he prepared for his European holiday, he resolved not to struggle to attain office; it would possibly come in any event without effort; but to study to be able to use it efficiently and nobly when it came. In the meantime he aimed at forming alliances with men of capacity and honour, and at dealing with the public questions of the day from an independent position.

Literature was an abiding interest; for writing his faculties were fittest, he thought, and he yearned for what he saw as the accompaniment of a literary life, the enjoyment of a select circle of friends such as used to meet at his table in Dublin in the 'forties. Friends were essential to his happiness; his soul only overflowed in genial talk among con-

genial associates. This made the call of Ireland all the more
insistent; there were half a dozen friends there for whose
company he craved; if he could only see them again he felt
he could be content with Australia for the rest of his life.

He had another reason for going home. He wanted to
consult the Jesuits in Stonyhurst about the education of his
boys—the eldest had been there since 1855—and to see
something of the European continent. Although " I am not
sure," he said, " that the excursions I look forward to with
most pleasure are not trips to Howth and Bray with a few
old friends." He had kept in touch with Irish affairs through
correspondence with Thomas O'Hagan and John Blake
Dillon. He had heard of the unexpected death of Smith
O'Brien, " one of the most upright and disinterested men I
ever encountered in life ;" and of the plan to erect a
national monument to O'Connell, a project which Dillon,
the honorary secretary, had interested him in.

He got the warmest of welcomes on landing in England
from old parliamentary friends, some of whom offered him
their houses and servants, and met some of the up and coming Irish political figures, among them Blake, the new member for Waterford, a Young Irelander a little out-of-date,
and The O'Donoghue who, in concert with G. H. Moore,
then represented the extreme wing of Nationalists.
O'Donoghue told him about the Fenians, of John Mitchel's
distrust of Moore and Moore's distrust of Dillon. " Alas and
alas," he cried, " for the once proud people of Banba." His
literary conversations were more rewarding. He had the
satisfaction of meeting Robert Browning whom he regarded
as the first poet of his age and country and of finding that
whereas he habitually disparaged the Catholic Church in his
poems he shared Duffy's view that cognisance should be
taken of the fact that the Catholic Church was the Church
of the Irish people and the Protestant Church the Church
of the English people and that the Protestant Church in

Ireland should therefore be disestablished. He was entertained at a public dinner at St. James's Hall, London, which curiously revived the main incidents of his life. John Dillon, a co-founder of *The Nation*, sat by his side. Sir John Gray who had been tried with O'Connell and Duffy in 1843 was there also, as well as D'Arcy McGee who had shared with Duffy the trials and dangers of 1848. Sir Colman O'Loghlen to whose legal skill he largely owed his subsequent triumphant emergence from his unprecedented tussle with the State sat nearby, while all around were the survivors of the Independent Party of 1852 augmented by recent recruits who adhered to the same principles.

Duffy had naturally wanted to get over to Ireland as soon as possible and was bombarded by welcoming messages. One particularly warm one came from Father Tom O'Shea, one of the Callan curates. " My darling Duffy," he wrote, " welcome, welcome to Ireland—would that I could say to home, but still welcome—you have a home in every honest Irish heart." And when he got to Dublin with his wife and daughter in June, 1865, he was plunged into affairs as if he had only been out of the country for a week. At a dinner one evening with Dillon, Ferguson, D. F. McCarthy, John O'Hagan, P. J. Smyth and other old associates the only stranger in the company, Prendergast, the author of the book on the Cromwellian Settlement, told a story of how at Ballingarry he had found that the conflict in which Smith O'Brien was involved had taken place in a cabbage garden, a phrase which stuck. Duffy, offended like the others, promptly told Prendergast that if he wanted to disparage a generous gentleman, he ought to do so somewhere else than among that gentleman's most intimate friends.

D'Arcy McGee, who had risen to be Minister for Agriculture in the Canadian Government, was in Ireland for the International Exhibition being held in Dublin but had not been invited to the dinner because of a speech he had

recently delivered in Wexford, his home town, which gave
wide offence. "I was one of the Young Ireland Fighters of
1848," he declared. "I am not at all ashamed of Young
Ireland. Why should I be? Politically we were a pack of
fools, but we were honest in our folly and no man need
blush at forty for the follies of one and twenty, unless he
still perseveres in them, having no longer the fair excuse to
plead of youth and inexperience." And speaking of the
Fenians whose exploits in Canada had inspired him with a
hatred of their organisation he said: "Some of these seem to
think that as I was a Young Irelander some twenty years
ago I ought to show some leniency for them. Why, Young
Ireland, as I am free to say, was politically a folly, but the
men were honest and manly. Men like Thomas Davis and
Duffy and others still living would have scorned to range
themselves with these Punch and Judy Jacobins whose sole
scheme of action seems to be to get their heads broken."
Duffy had always had a deep affection for McGee but this
was more than he could endure, so he wrote him a letter in
which he said he preferred him as a fool at twenty than as
the philosopher and statesman he had become at forty.
McGee was to pay the price for his outspokenness; and for
his subsequent abandonment of Repeal in favour of a union
of equal peoples. In April, 1868, he was assassinated in
Ottawa by a Fenian who may or may not have been acting
under instructions.

By that time the Fenians had risen, first prematurely and
abortively in Kerry in February, 1867, and then more
deliberately but equally abortively the following month.
The bishops had publicly pronounced against them for
several years and the Kerry outbreak drew from Duffy's
"most generous and considerate" friend, Moriarty,
the bishop of the diocese, a particularly savage but frequently misquoted denunciation of the heads of the organisation. For them, he said, "we must acknowledge that

eternity is not long enough nor hell hot enough to punish such miscreants ". Cullen, so much Duffy's villain of the piece, met this situation with an appeal for justice for Ireland which would deprive the false patriotism of the Fenians of its appeal. Privately he deplored Moriarty's " foolish exaggeration " and suggested to a Roman correspondent that he should be called to account for it. He may, of course, like so many other people, not have noticed that Moriarty was concentrating on men like James Stephens who had absorbed revolutionary Socialist ideas on the Continent and who, he alleged, from safe billets in Paris and New York were urging young Irishmen to put their lives in jeopardy.

Dillon brought Duffy up-to-date about the growth of Fenianism which had drawn many of the ex-Confederates into its ranks. They both agreed that the conspirators were honest men but that the task they had set themselves was beyond their capabilities. Dillon sounded him about returning to Irish political life which meant joining the National Association which had been formed in December, 1864, and of which, in an unusual combination, Dillon, the '48 man, was the honorary secretary and Cardinal Cullen the most active promoter. This Association was intended to provide Irishmen with a constitutional alternative to Fenianism, and its programme emphasised the need to disestablish the Protestant Church, to effect land reform and to achieve State-aided denominational education. Cullen had always been firmly convinced that politics were not the direct concern of bishops and priests but he had changed his view when he saw the growth of Fenianism among a people frustrated by the divisions that followed the failure of the Tenant League and the continuing absence of justice for Catholics. He had been helped to arrive at this view by among others the Lord Mayor of Dublin, Peter Paul McSwiney, who came close to Cullen's ideal of the Catholic politician. A General Election was at hand and Dillon thought that the Association might become the genuine Irish Party that Duffy had predicted in 1849.

Duffy was tempted to say ' yes ' to this offer but he wanted to be assured that Dr. Cullen would raise no difficulties and that George Henry Moore and the popular priests of the Tenant League would join the movement. Dillon assured him that there was no difficulty so far as Cullen was concerned and at a Catholic University dinner he went to, Duffy was welcomed cordially on behalf of a number of ecclesiastics who habitually acted with Cullen. On the other hand he found Moore bitterly opposed to any political association with Cullen and his friends who had done so much, he insisted, to destroy one of the greatest national movements Ireland had ever possessed. And when Duffy consulted the Tenant League priests he found them as rootedly opposed as Moore was to any co-operation with an organisation of which Cullen was a member. They were backing John Martin whose constitutional agitation for Repeal through an organisation called the Irish National League was making no headway. Their opposition was bad enough but Duffy discovered that Moore was also prejudiced against Dillon who had Duffy's complete confidence. Not unnaturally therefore he decided to go back to Australia ; he thought it unwise that any Irishman—even Dr. Cullen— should be shut out of public life who was not charged with dishonesty or corruption. But before he left Ireland he helped Dillon to fight and win the Tipperary constituency. He regarded it, however, as a " significant illustration of the senseless and stupid policy which the Fenians borrowed from the Chartists that a Fenian mob in the capital of the county silenced by clamour the most distinguished and best-tested nationalist in the country." Duffy thought that the means and methods of the Fenians were insensate, though he admired their courage and devotion, and on his return to Melbourne he strongly discountenanced agitation in their favour. He dreamed constantly of the Fenian prisoners sleeping in stone cells and particularly of men of culture like O'Leary, Kickham and O'Keeffe who were deprived both of books and of pen and ink. " It would be a good action," he told John O'Hagan in the beginning of 1866, " if you, who would be listened to, would ask Mr. Gladstone, who has told us his opinion of the treatment proper for State prisoners, to allow them books and pen and ink, and a few yards of matting for their cells. They would not be less secure, but they would be rescued from torture."

In what was left to him of his holiday Duffy saw Rome under the guidance of Father Tom Burke, the Irish Dominican orator, and had a private audience with the Pope, Gregory XVI. In London he discussed Australian politics with Disraeli, and in Paris he tried, but without success, to see Montalembert, who was his ideal of what a Catholic gentleman should be—genuinely pious and a strict disciplinarian but entirely free from bigotry or intolerance. It was in Paris, too, that he wrote a new preface for the thirty-ninth edition of his *Ballad Poetry of Ireland*. This was still selling like hot cakes: in twenty years no less than 76,000 copies of it had found buyers wherever the English language was used.

About this time, too, he completed the entries in a scrapbook which he entitled *Ars Vitae*. This had been begun many years before and had been recast and revised in December, 1864. This little volume was intended for his own eyes only and was written in order to help him, he said, to make the best of his fundamental character and to turn his physical constitution and natural inclinations to good account. " Believe me," he wrote, addressing himself, " what you need is a plan of life;" and one of the points of the particular plan he devised for himself was to avoid living in the future, which might be short enough anyhow, and to enjoy the present, day by day, with his family. The only

ark of refuge from the storms of the world was Home. But
when he practised the habit of seclusion he found that his
influence waned. The Australian public wanted more, not
less, of him; they even complained of his wife not visiting
them. She had more than enough to do with her own young
family, and, highly cultivated as she was, she never found
Australian company to her liking.

The shape of *Ars Vitae* is interesting. It sets out Duffy's
aims in life, and the elements for the enjoyment of life. This
is followed by three sections on relations with other people
whom he divided into friends, opponents and neutrals; and
these in turn are followed by sections on the faculties to be
cultivated, the training of the intellect etc. Before and after
the plentiful quotations from obviously exceptionally wide
reading, and sometimes interwoven through them, are passages of self-criticism. For instance: " I am too much
accustomed to rely upon unreal and impossible conditions
of happiness. Before I came here (to Australia) I longed for
the peace of a new home where I could be obscure without
reproach or active without being dogged with ancient
enmities; forgetting that I would soon have new friends and
new enemies with all the train of consequences. Again I
have sometimes in this country pictured to myself the repose
of a home in Wicklow or Versailles with no more active
duties in life; but without active duties, life would have no
active enjoyments and would probably be dull to the verge
of suicide ". "A neglected duty or even a postponed one," he
writes elsewhere, " hangs on me with a dull sense of pain . . .
which spoils leisure or enjoyment. Before you are happy for
an hour your conscience must be satisfied ".

In the section on dealing with friends Duffy looked about
him for examples to be imitated or avoided. Thus : " Dingly
(an Australian politician) with his remarkable talents and
information, would be a man of political importance if a
demonstrative self-conceit and petulance did not ruin all.

Suppose him as modest and reticent as John O'Hagan, or forgetful of self as Davis and systematically self-sacrificing as W. G. (Wilson Gray) was, in this country he would be a power, potentate and dominion. Hence for public ends one must offer the sacrifice of some private one, or but imperfectly succeed . . . Remember Davis's cordial frank helpful treatment of his associates and the result. And his singular reserve in speaking of others; his generous interpretation of men's actions and motives. And O'Hagan's cordiality which no pressure of business or uncertainty of health or personal trouble disturbed. And on the other hand, . . . Il Vero's (Carlyle) want of charity for his contemporaries and associates ". Friends were essential to Duffy's happiness. Speaking to himself he said : " Your soul ordinarily repressed only overflows in genial talk among congenial associates ".

In the section on dealing with opponents Duffy remembered with pain how much time he lost in Parliament—he was thinking of Victoria only—in making, proving or rebutting personal charges. Mentioning some instances, he goes on : " How little tranquillity in my life and though I believe I was right on each occasion, how much rashness and want of temper so many angry controversies argue. I have often refused to be interrupted in debate by an explanation, and rightly too, but have commonly done it fiercely and peremptorily; whereas the refusal would have been equally effective clothed in the most courteous language and uttered in the gentlest tones . . . Higginbotham once said in the *Argus* that it was my demeanour in the House which made me so many enemies; which was substantially true I fear ". And later on he writes in the scrapbook that " till a man has learned to conquer himself he need count on no other conquest ". " Remember O'Connell's patience with opposition in committee; Davis's open unruffled demeanour in argument; Dillon's placidity under contradiction and Pigot's unshakeable good humour ".

This self-criticism and the doubtless sporadic efforts at reform that followed it confirm the judgment of the Australian historian, Geoffrey Serle, which sees nobility and great charm struggling within Duffy against pettiness, petulance and egotism. Serle sees him as a largely disinterested reformer, with little inclination for money-making, a liberal of the classic variety with a dash of utopianism in his make-up who could rise to greatness in tackling great problems and in attaining the highest political office and who yet never fulfilled his great promise. The same writer quotes a critic of Duffy's who attributed his sour temper to adversity, and he himself suggests that the adversity in question derived from Duffy's Irish background which condemned him to fight battle after battle against prejudice which could never be borne down. But while it is doubtless true that adversity played on his passionate nature, there is no evidence that we know of that it turned him sour. Duffy loved and hated strongly, but it was not his habit to retire into himself and growl unprofitably about the state of things. His temper was of the explosive kind.

16

During his two years' absence in Europe, the coalition government of Victoria had acquired, in Duffy's opinion, a dubious character, maintaining their power largely by political corruption and by setting at naught for selfish ends some of the main principles of the Constitution. Duffy was not a member of parliament at this time but in the summer of 1867 when he was back in Melbourne the constituency of Dalhousie fell vacant and an invitation to become a candidate was so largely signed that he had no difficulty in accepting it. It was an immense territory and Duffy did not welcome the prospect of having to speak at the meetings his committee arranged for him. He usually came away disgusted from any public meeting he had to address. Michie, who was the leading advocate at the Melbourne Bar, once told him that he was the best debater he had ever listened to, but not a good speech-maker; Wilson Gray, a former editor of the *Freeman's Journal*, had described his statement of a case as a trail of intellectual light, but Duffy himself believed that all his set speeches were bad and were not improved by his incurably bad voice. It was this deficiency which made him cultivate a conversational tone, modelling himself on Macaulay, Disraeli, McGee, Bright and Davis who were among the best speakers he had heard.

As always, his own countrymen supported him zealously. At a meeting in support of his opponent at which Duffy was called an Irish rebel and an Irish papist they rushed the platform and had to be restrained by Duffy who reminded them that he had been in fact described with great accuracy; what was he anyway but an Irish rebel and an Irish papist?

He was duly elected. In the interim he had busied himself in opposing the Government's constitutional, financial and educational policies and had been particularly successful in forcing the withdrawal of a plan to suppress the denominational schools and to provide for the teaching of something described as religion without dogma in the State schools. The Government ultimately fell on a proposal to impose a property tax which Duffy also strenuously opposed; and the Governor called on Duffy to form a Cabinet.

The first three men he communicated with suggested that he should put a respectable nonentity at the head of the Government, Duffy himself taking any other place he thought proper. They made this suggestion to avoid the rooted prejudice against having an Irish Catholic in that position. Duffy replied that he would see the Parliament of Victoria in hell before he would consent to denigrate his race and people by permitting the Emancipation Act to be repealed in his person. " I washed my hands of these feeble friends ", he told Cashel Hoey, " and I had the audacity for the first time to place three Catholics! " There were cries of " no Popery ", yells mingled with a laugh of derision, but his policy speech brought the vast bulk of the people on his side, and changed the tone of the entire press.

He assumed office in 1871 with high intentions, among them the establishment of new industries suitable to a southern soil and climate and drawing their labour force in part from the foundlings of the State and from the army of indolent and dangerous men in jail who through the opportunity of earning their daily bread might be capable of being reformed. The land question which had always been his care had been ruined, he believed, by maladministration and clamoured for attention, as did the public finances which were then in a state of confusion and which Duffy was committed to restoring to order without imposing an additional burden on industry. Nothing had hitherto been done to feed the imagination of the people which had never soared beyond the level of provincial mediocrity. He proposed, accordingly, to establish an art museum, because he had learned from his travels that by the aid of art, history and political science could be taught as well as an appreciation of aesthetics. He was determined, moreover, to ensure that no reproach could be made against his Government on the score of the exercise of patronage. The London *Spectator* declared that they had read nothing better for years than the manifesto in which Duffy set out his proposals. This had been prepared, the journal said, by this typical man of a class which the English said could never govern nor be governed. He was the sort of man for whom the Tories in England were sighing, " the born administrator, utterly free of flummery and buncombe, clear as to his ends, clearer still as to his means, ready to compromise anything except principle, but giving even to compromise an impression of original force."

He successfully withstood the first major Opposition attack which alleged that he had, at an inter-colony conference on tariffs, accepted propositions that were inimical to the interests of Victoria. Fellows, the leader of the Opposition, had seasoned his speech with suggestions reflecting on Duffy's Irish past and this drew from Duffy a typical riposte : " I will soon have to account for my whole life," he said, " and I feel that it has been defaced by many sins and shortcomings; but there is one portion of it I must except from this censure. I can say without fear, without impiety, when I am called before the Judge of all men, I shall not fear to answer for my Irish career. I did what I believed best for Ireland, without any relation to its effects on myself. I am challenged to justify myself for having been an Irish rebel, under penalty of your fatal censure; and am content to reply that the recollection that when my native country was in mortal peril I was among those who staked life for her deliverance, is a memory I would not exchange for anything that parliaments or sovereigns can give or take away."

Duffy's government fell in 1872 to the united opposition's second onslaught, and sardonically enough on the issue of political jobbery. The cases cited were rather trifling except two, and Duffy disposed of the first of these, the filling of a vacancy for a piermastership by his Minister of Railways, by showing that the backers of the appointed man included five members of the Opposition. The other case was more difficult for it involved Duffy personally as well as an intimate friend of his, Cashel Hoey, who on his recommendation had been appointed secretary to the Agent General of Victoria in London. Hoey had been the editor of *The Nation* for some time after Duffy's departure for Australia and later had become a member of the English bar. His competence was not in doubt, but though Duffy made the best case he could otherwise for the appointment, he was not convincing. The Government was defeated and Hoey lost his job. Duffy sought to reverse the vote by an appeal to the country but the Governor refused to dissolve Parliament and a combination of Free-Traders, Protectionists and squatters under J. G. Francis took over.

In the fatal division that put Duffy out of office a couple of his supporters abstained, and two others voted with the Opposition, one of them under the influence of O'Shanassy who by now had become a prosperous landholder in New South Wales and was more vindictively antagonistic to Duffy than ever before. Duffy, cut to the quick by these desertions, availed of a bye-election to defeat one of those who had left him as well as an O'Shanassy candidate.

In 1873 he was invited to accept a knighthood. To have refused, as he was tempted to do in the atmosphere of disagreement with the Governor, would, his colleagues thought, have been misunderstood. Fundamentally he had no objection to receiving this particular distinction or the Companionship of the Order of St. Michael and St. George that was conferred on him later; he would have done so in Ireland if she, like the State of Victoria, had a native Parliament and Government of her own. That was how his old champion, Father Doyle, saw it too. The title had been fairly won in a free country, he said, but in Ireland Sir Charles Gavan Duffy would continue to be best known simply as Duffy.

17

By being out of office Duffy was able to return to Europe for the second time. He travelled alone on this occasion, and landed at Brindisi on a lovely spring day in 1875 with the intention of spending a long holiday doing absolutely nothing. His health was again causing him concern and he had lost his voice. He went to Paris a few times, and then to London to see a specialist. In Paris he was invited to a reception at the Elysée. The President, Marshal MacMahon, he found " very Irish—large, frank, fiery " and among the company some of the old Irish—a Nugent, an O'Brien, an O'Neill—who could scarcely speak a word of English. This surprised Duffy who asked a Captain MacDermott who was also in the group why he did not continue to speak English in memory of his ancestors. " Monsieur," said the Captain, " when my ancestors lived in their native country they spoke their native tongue." The reply pleased Duffy. *Vive MacDermott!* he wrote in his diary.

On his visits to Paris he also saw much of John O'Leary, who had been released from prison on condition that he lived abroad. Duffy found him a Fenian of a class he had never seen before, and rarely afterwards; moderate in opinion, generally just to his opponents, and entirely without passion or enthusiasm except a devoted love of Ireland. He was a great reader of books, and Duffy feared, a great dreamer of dreams. He had been a confederate in '48 and had become something of an anti-clerical as a result of the opposition of the priests to the Young Ireland movement. While mildly critical of Duffy's policy at the time of the formation of the Tenant League he became rather attached to him, and after his return to Dublin introduced some of the new generation to him. Katherine Tynan describes an occasion in the late eighties when O'Leary brought herself, Rose Kavanagh, the editor of the *Irish Fireside* and Stephen Gwynn to the Shelbourne Hotel to meet " the great man ". Duffy had written an unfavourable opinion of Katherine's early poems to Father Matthew Russell, S.J., of *The Irish Monthly* and she had retaliated in a " careless " speech. She thought he might have been more pleased had he known she could repeat some of his " ringing ballads ".

On the occasion of his first visit to Ireland during this second European holiday he had conversations with leading priests of the former Tenant League who were anxious that he should go into Parliament but he could do little more than consult them because of his throat condition for which a London specialist recommended a stay at Aix les Bains. His voice showing no improvement he settled down on the coast at Cannes, Mentone and Monte Carlo for the winter. He amused himself looking at the English visitors and listening to their prattle. " I fear I am growing an old fogey," he told his wife in a letter. " There was a family stopping here recently consisting of the grandson and granddaughter of Lord Thurlow, Chancellor under George III. The lady asked me if I knew her grandfather. I replied that I did not, but that the fault was not mine, as he had placed an impediment in the way of our acquaintance by dying before I was born." Another English family staying in the same hotel with Duffy spoke of all the places they had visited by their foreign names. They had come from " la Belgique " by way of " la Suisse " and proposed to visit " l'Autriche " in the summer. Duffy suggested that there was an interesting island lying north of " la France " which might occupy some leisure months agreeably, " l'Angleterre."

It was here on the Riviera that he saw in the newspapers
that John Martin had died on the 29th March, 1875, within
days of attending the funeral of his brother-in-law John
Mitchel, and a telegram came from some Meath priests
shortly afterwards inviting him to stand for the parliamentary vacancy. Duffy replied that he had no desire to
re-enter Irish politics ; in any event the medical treatment
he was undergoing made it impossible for him to travel to
Ireland immediately ; but if he were nominated he would
feel it his patriotic duty to go forward. He explained that
he was still a Repealer, holding the principles he had
shared with O'Connell, Smith O'Brien, Dillon, Davis and
Meagher and he would do his best in concert with the Irish
Members to serve the Irish cause, but he would not join the
Home Rule Association now being led by Isaac Butt. He
failed to get the nomination, however, which went to Charles
Stewart Parnell, a shy, stuttering, cricket-playing young
squire from the County Wicklow.

Duffy did not like Butt because of his rejection of the idea
of Independent Opposition and the danger that he was again
making possible the practice of place-begging and sub-
serviency to English Governments ; but he might not have
worried unduly for already the beginning of a change was
to be seen of which he would have approved, although the
methods to effect it might not have been those he would
have chosen. Within a short time of his election to the
Meath constituency young Parnell reacted against the club
atmosphere of the House of Commons and associated himself with a group of Irish obstructionists. This was the pre-
lude to the ousting of Butt from the leadership of the Home
Rule League and to a vigorously independent policy *vis-à-
vis* English political parties the like of which had never been
seen in Westminster. Before this occurred, however, an
unsuccessful effort to displace Butt was made from a different quarter. The Lord Mayor of Dublin, P. P. MacSwiney,

prompted by P. J. Smyth, tried to establish a Party in opposition to him during the O'Connell centenary celebrations in 1875, a development of which Duffy became fully aware when he again went over to Dublin in August of that year to attend the O'Connell centenary celebrations. These promised to be a triumphant success, with deputations coming from all over Ireland and from the Catholic countries on the Continent.

Duffy had planned to spend about a month in Ireland, staying with friends, visiting his mother's grave, and taking a look at places that were part of his personal history, Merton, in the Sandford Road district of Dublin, where he had lived. Richmond Jail and what was left of Newgate and the old *Nation* offices. What a sweep there had been in a few years—Dillon, Moore, Mitchel, Martin, and others he named were all dead since he was there last. In Merton, he told his wife, he found some people who had recently purchased it, in possession. " I went up to a grave old lady . . . took off my hat and told her that this house had great interest for me, as it was here I brought home my young wife long ago. The old lady was quite touched by such a sentiment, and carried me to every part of the house and grounds. Perhaps she was once a young bride but it was long ago. Everyone asked whether you were in London or Paris and could scarcely be persuaded that you were in Melbourne. So that I had to announce that I was going to rejoin you there forthwith, or I would probably have been ducked in the Liffey—for this is a very chivalrous nation."

During the celebrations at which Duffy represented the Irish in Melbourne, MacSwiney told him of his political intentions. He was supported, he said, by Dr. Cullen, now a Cardinal, who had promised a substantial portion of the necessary capital for a new daily paper and he invited Duffy to remain at home and take charge of the whole enterprise. The Cardinal had entirely changed his opinion about Duffy's Irish policy, he said. "Alas," said Duffy, "I have not changed my opinion about his. To ask me to direct a newspaper, whose funds are to be largely furnished by Dr. Cullen, is to ask me to make a voyage certain to end in shipwreck, and I respectfully decline." Earlier, an eccentric acquaintance of his, Tristram Gregg, who had at one time been Grand Chaplain of the Orange Order, asked him for an introduction to the Archbishop. He believed he had discovered how to confer immortality without the intervention of death and wanted distinguished subjects to practise on. Cullen would be able, he claimed, to remain Archbishop for more centuries than had elapsed since the coming of Saint Patrick. "Good gracious," said Duffy, "you frighten me; that's just what I don't want to happen. If you are going to inflict Dr. Cullen on us in perpetuity, I must decline your immortality." But banteringly he added that he would not object to a century or two in *good* company.

The night before his conversation with MacSwiney Duffy witnessed an unpleasant demonstration of the growth of factionism. The Lord Mayor's party had opposed all efforts to give Butt a prominent place in the centenary celebrations, while another led by A. M. Sullivan insisted upon it as his right. The result was that at a public meeting an oration composed by Duffy's life-long friend, Thomas, now Lord Chancellor O'Hagan was shouted down, and when at a banquet Duffy himself rose to speak to the toast of Irish Nationality, cries of "Butt! Butt!" forced him to resume his seat. The Lord Mayor's efforts from the chair to control the clamour only made it worse. Butt, who was sitting next to Duffy, said he would put an end to the trouble if Duffy would induce the Lord Mayor to give him a moment's hearing, but Duffy, disgusted with both parties for destroying a noble national demonstration, refused to interfere. After a while the principal guests, including Duffy, withdrew from the room; and the Lord Mayor ordered the gas to be turned off, so that "what would have been a strength and honour to Ireland became a disgrace."

After that chilling experience it must have been a relief to Duffy to return to the sunny Mediterranean on the first stage of the long journey back to Australia. A. M. Sullivan had tried to make amends by explaining to the public that there were probably not a dozen men at the banquet who had recognised Duffy but his words can have given Duffy little satisfaction with their implication that he had become a back-number in Irish politics. At Monaco a sculptor was waiting to make a bust of him and Thomas O'Hagan hurried out from London to spend a few days in his company. Duffy had been surprised and pained by the arguments O'Hagan used in his centenary oration to justify O'Connell's violence towards some of his opponents: he thought that they might be employed to justify the methods Butt and his friends had recently used at Dublin. Duffy's attitude to O'Connell had not changed with the passing of the years. "The O'Connell you paint," he told O'Hagan, "is as ideal a person as King Arthur of Tennyson. He was no more the generous, single-minded, unselfish hero of your prose idyll than he was the impostor ordinarily presented in *The Times* —but a strange compound of both." He had commended O'Hagan earlier for his charge and address to Captain Mackay, the Irish-American Fenian, when he appeared before him in the dock. "I am not sure that any other judge would have the courage to treat a Fenian prisoner as a fellow-creature, a man of capacity and honour, and inferentially a patriot . . . The stale and stupid lie that all these men of Irish blood and feeling who left a prosperous country . . . for what was plainly a forlorn hope, are merely robbers in pursuit of loot and plunder outrages common sense. We would not believe it of Italians, Hungarians, or Poles, and nobody did believe it of the Fenians, however solemnly it was enunciated . . ." But Duffy added that they had been taught by spies, informers and assassinations like that of D'Arcy McGee, that the Fenians were not all Captain Mackays.

18

The final stage of Duffy's Australian career lasted four years, from 1876 to 1880. As always he experienced no difficulty in finding a constituency and returning to Parliament, although bronchitis which he had contracted during the return voyage prevented him from taking part in the election campaign. Within a few months there was a dissolution ; Duffy was re-elected, and the Party to which he belonged, led by Graham Berry, became the Government of Victoria. Berry offered Duffy any office in the Government he might wish to have but Duffy considered it inappropriate for a man who had been Prime Minister to act in a secondary position. By agreement between the principal Parties he was then chosen to be the Speaker of the House and the duties were not onerous for one with his experience of Parliamentary procedure.

He had leisure now for a task he had long envisaged, the writing of the story of Young Ireland; and this work was substantially advanced by 1880 when he retired from the political scene and returned to Europe. " I should probably have finished my life on the scene which had occupied so large a section of it," he wrote, " but that I loathed the task of answering again and again the insensate inventions of religious bigotry. It was a favourite theory with Orangemen and Conservatives that I could not resist the tendency to sacrifice my public duties to some inscrutable interest of the Pope, and though no one had ever produced a single fact to support the hypothesis, and though I exorcised the evil spirit whenever it appeared, yet, it seemed to me a pitiful waste of life even to conquer in such encounters. I determined that

my public career would end here. . . ." Australia had been
uncommonly kind to him, but he had made ample recom-
pense in public service of a high order. His name is recorded
among the founders of the State of Victoria and his children
served the Commonwealth with great distinction. His eldest
son, John, was a Cabinet Minister in Victoria, his second
eldest son, Frank, became Chief Justice of the High Court
of Australia and was knighted—as was a son of *his,* Charles
Gavan Duffy, Judge of the Supreme Court of Victoria.
Duffy's third son became Clerk of the Houses of Parliament
of Victoria, and a fourth, Philip, a pioneer in railway engin-
eering in Western Australia. It has been said recently, however, by the Australian historian already quoted that while
Duffy himself rose close to greatness in tackling great
problems, and was Premier, Speaker, and a member of four
governments in Victoria, his Australian career was an anti-
climax in that he never fulfilled his great promise. But if
anti-climax there was it may be that Duffy was never entirely
reconciled to being an Australian and nothing else; he was
first and foremost an Irishman, and was never able to give
his whole mind to Australian problems. And even in Australia he laboured to ensure that there Irishmen would avail
as fully as possible of their opportunities where more than
anywhere else on earth Irishmen had attained so open and
successful a career.

Because of bronchitis Duffy, on retirement, went to live
in Nice on the French Riviera, and there in various villas, or
in a large comfortable flat and with a pension of £1,000 a
year—good money in those days—he was able to finish the
Young Ireland book and to shape some others that had long
been floating in his mind. His wife, Susan, had died of a
slow consumption in September, 1878. They had been together for over thirty years, and she had borne him eleven
children of whom six—three boys and three girls had survived. A couple of years later, in 1880, he married a niece

of hers, the lovely red-haired musical Louise Hall, the daughter of George Hall, of Rock Ferry, Cheshire. There was a great disparity in their ages; he was sixty-four and she in her twenties ; but he loved her and she returned his love and was proud to be the wife of so great a man. She had four children at the time of her death in 1889—George, Louise, Bryan and Tom — and these were reared by the daughters of the second marriage, Susan, Harriet, and Geraldine who came from Australia to keep house for their father. Bryan and Tom left home when young to be priests. Bryan, as a Jesuit, spent more than twenty years in South Africa at his selfless task as an Inspector of Religious Instruction, and his work as a writer and preacher earned him an enduring reputation. Tom became a member of the Paris Missionary Society, and was sent to India. He re-energised Catholic life in the Archdiocese of Pondicherry through the training of catechists for whom he provided a central residential Training College. George grew up in the law, married A. M. Sullivan's daughter, Margaret, defended Sir Roger Casement for his life, was one of the negotiators of the Anglo-Irish Treaty in 1921 and was Ireland's Minister for Foreign Affairs before becoming the President of the Irish High Court. Louise, Duffy's youngest daughter, became an Irish language pioneer, taught in Pearse's Scoil Íde, took part in the 1916 Rising, and was afterwards the founder and headmistress of a remarkable school, Scoil Bhríde. She is a Master of Arts and Honorary Doctor of Laws of the National University of Ireland, and an untiring worker in the Legion of Mary.

She remembers her father as a bearded, less than middle-sized figure who always gave her two kisses when she bade him good-night, one for herself, the other for her dead mother whose name she bore. He took it as a matter of course that his sons should get first place and the gold medal in all their examinations. But when Louise did this he gave her ten francs which for her was an absolute fortune; she had never possessed all of ten francs before.   George was struck by this display of favouritism and after the fashion of the loyal son in the parable he said to Louise, " I've been winning firsts for years and he never gave me anything." But George remained the pet nevertheless, and his father took pains to form him and direct him towards a career.

Young Ireland, Duffy's most important work, first appeared in 1880 and the story, and its aftermath, was continued in *Four Years of Irish History* and in the *League of North and South* which were published within the next six years. These books, it is generally conceded, have left the historians deeply in Duffy's debt although they have recently been considered " flagrantly partial " in the chapters that deal with the major conflicts in Duffy's Irish career.   Taken together the praise and the criticism indicate that there is room for a reappraisal of the historical position of O'Connell, Davis and Mitchel, and of Duffy himself.   O'Connell in particular remains undoubtedly and unfairly under a cloud and for this Duffy and Mitchel bear responsibility. In Duffy's history, as Lecky said, O'Connell always appears as half patriot, half charlatan, a man of amazing abilities, and in many respects in advance of his time, but untruthful, rapacious, unscrupulous, overbearing, and very rarely acting through motives that were purely single-minded and disinterested.   In so behaving towards O'Connell, Duffy and Mitchel were both influenced to some extent by Carlyle who detested and despised " The big Beggarman ".   Duffy has also been blamed for being too modest, for not taking anything like enough credit for his own contribution to the Irish cause.

In 1882, Duffy also released *A Bird's Eye View of Irish History*, a chapter taken from *Young Ireland*, and some years later his life of *Thomas Davis* and his *Conversations with Carlyle*. His last major work was the two volume biography he called *My Life in Two Hemispheres ;* this was dated

1898. In addition to these works he prepared a short life of Davis (1895) and wrote a number of articles and lectures on constitutional, agrarian, and literary subjects. The most important of these at the time was *A Fair Constitution for Ireland* which was published in the *Contemporary Review*, printed as a pamphlet and then widely quoted from. This was produced in the context of what became known as the Carnarvon Controversy in which Duffy played a singular part which he described in the elaborate chapter he later contributed to Barry O'Brien's *Life of Parnell*. O'Brien spent three weeks with Duffy in the autumn in 1898. Duffy was then 83, but youthful in mind and manner, a most genial host and the pleasantest of companions. O'Brien also thought he was the best raconteur he had ever met, with a keen sense of humour and a caustic wit. Doubtless they talked unendingly of Parnell and the latest might-have-been of Irish history.

Duffy had made Parnell's acquaintance in the spring of 1880 and had been questioned by him as to his political intentions. Duffy had replied that he wanted as always to work for Ireland but not in Parliament and, moreover, that he desired to keep himself free of parties. During the following five stormy years, he watched Parnell's career mainly from a distance but his annual visits to London and Dublin gave him opportunities of conversing with a man who more than anyone he had ever known possessed a mastery of a race among whom individuality was a passion. And he saw that this proud, isolated dictator achieved his authority without any of the gifts that had characterised his predecessors. For his part Parnell had a high regard for Duffy. Publicly and privately he alluded gratefully to his role in the creation of Independent Opposition in 1852 which was the frail forerunner of his own monolithic Parliamentary Party and was on that account, perhaps, prepared to listen to criticisms of his failure to control the excesses of the land agitation. Duffy,

for his part, refrained from criticising the particular trans-
actions of the Irish Party of which he did not approve
because, he said, " I thought their enemies in front ought
never to be supplemented by auxiliaries from behind."

When the Phoenix Park murders occurred in 1882, Parnell
was so horrified that he announced his intention of resign-
ing and suggested to his immediate entourage that Duffy
should be asked to take his place. One wonders what Duffy
would have done if this request had been made to him ; he
seems to have had a rooted objection at this time to returning to Parliament which would have meant spending the
winters in London and he refused invitations to stand for
the Monaghan constituency in 1885 and 1892. Also he was,
he said, a simple Repealer. The question of becoming the
leader of the Party however came to nothing in 1882.
Parnell changed his mind and three years later because
of utter dissatisfaction with the Liberals from whom
the Irish had traditionally expected most, he helped to overthrow them and to set up the Tories under Salisbury in their
stead. The question of what return the Tories were to make
for this gift from the gods focussed attention on Lord
Carnarvon, the Lord Lieutenant for Ireland in the new
administration.

Duffy had met Carnarvon when he was Secretary of
State for the Colonies and he now found him deeply
interested in a scheme for a Central Irish Parliament with
four provincial assemblies that Duffy had propounded in an
article in which he appealed to the Conservatives to carry
Home Rule. Carnarvon had had the article printed in the
Conservative Party magazine and had brought it to
Salisbury's notice. Following some correspondence Duffy
went to Dublin to see Carnarvon and was immediately
invited to an official dinner at the Castle and to conversations in the Viceregal Lodge, but while the latter took
place immediately he excused himself from going to the

Castle because of a promise he had made long before never to enter its portals until it was occupied by a National Government. Carnarvon, who was finding his colleagues unreceptive, was not prepared to pledge himself to Home Rule, and he doubted whether he could get agreement on an alternative Duffy suggested, namely, to promise a Select Committee of enquiry whose report might form the basis of future legislation. Another General Election was looming up and Duffy told Carnarvon that he had advised Parnell not to support Tory candidates unless Ireland was assured of a *quid pro quo*. There were some further comings and goings, including a strange meeting in an empty London house between Carnarvon and Parnell, but the election came without any undertakings being given on the Tory side, while Parnell's support for the Tories was rather lukewarm in view of an indication in Gladstone's speeches that a Home Rule solution might be expected from him. Gladstone was in fact returned to power and introduced his first Home Rule Bill which Duffy declared would be received with enthusiasm by the Irish race ; the colonial system it offered was " one of the most courageous and disinterested experiments in human history ". During the Second Reading debate Parnell, for Party gain, made public the strictly private negotiations with Carnarvon. This, to Duffy's mind, was something which Parnell should never have done. He regarded it as a dishonourable act in the same way perhaps as he looked on Mitchel's surrender of his parole.

In this hour of triumph for Parnell and his Party Duffy reminded them not to forget in their rejoicing how much they owed to their predecessors. Men rarely read old newspapers, he said; they behaved in politics as if they owed nothing to the men who had gone before them. Roger O'Moore was denied all control in the Confederation of Kilkenny which he had created, Wolfe Tone fell into disrepute, for moderation, with the United Irish Societies which he founded,

Grattan was denounced in the end by the Volunteers whom he had led to memorable victory, the Young Irelanders were expelled from the Repeal Association of which they were the most sincere and unselfish members, and even O'Connell lost his marvellous popularity. This reflection might teach all Irishmen to be modest. He recalled a story he had heard at his mother's knee and never forgotten. In a famine year a comfortable farmer was persuaded by his wife to send out his aged father to beg. The old man was equipped with a staff, a bag and half a blanket. After he was gone his frugal daughter-in-law enquired what had become of the other half of the blanket. After a long search it was found under the bed of her little boy. " Why, Mick, asthore, what did you want with a blanket ?" his father asked. " Father," said the boy, " I thought I'd keep it by me until I grew up to be a big man, and then it'll do for you when I send you out to beg." The time to beg comes to all political parties, sooner or later. Within five years of Duffy's warning the seemingly invincible party to which he addressed it crumbled as a result of Parnell's illicit affair with Kitty O'Shea and Ireland was torn asunder. A year later, Parnell, the uncrowned king, was dead. In the same year *The Nation,* which for long had been a mere shadow of its original brilliant self, ceased to have a separate existence.

19

The national upheaval that followed the O'Shea divorce proceedings grievously affected Duffy, of course, as it did all Irishmen, but he appears to have kept his feelings largely to himself and in public proposed a final burial of all national feuds, ancient and modern. His sympathies, however, were with the anti-Parnellite side, if only because for years he had considered Parnell too much of an autocrat; but in a pious family such as his, the name and repute of Kitty O'Shea could not be mentioned aloud so that the children grew up knowing little or nothing of what was happening. Duffy's youngest daughter Louise, still happily and actively with us, remembers the constant talk about Parnell and Gladstone whom, in her innocence, she conceived as two gladiators confronting each other in a large hall supported by gangs of noisy partisans. Then suddenly the name of Parnell dropped out of the conversation as if he had never existed; Louise did not know why. But he never ceased to deplore the disunion that followed Parnell's death, and when, after many years of frustration, a Unity Conference was proposed and he was suggested as a possible mediator he made it known that he was most willing to act provided that the three conflicting sections invited him to do so and assured him in advance that they would accept as final his decision whatever form it took. Redmond and Healy gave their consent but Dillon refused so that the idea was still-born.

Of course, as everybody knows, Gladstone's Home Rule efforts came to nothing; so did Duffy's " Fair Constitution " —a scheme of Government for Ireland—which he first pub-

lished in 1887 and republished in 1892. Parnell approved
of its main provisions for a bi-cameral parliament of paid
members with opportunity for minorities secured by a simple
form of Proportional Representation, and seats in the
Senate for ecclesiastics. The scheme was commended by,
amongst others, the Fenian John Boyle O'Reilly; but the
ecclesiastical provisions failed to win the support of Cardinal
Manning and Archbishop Walsh of Dublin. Gladstone would
not commit himself on the proposals as a whole although
some of his colleagues gave them " a frank and cordial
acceptance ". Duffy, as we have seen, had a high regard for
the Grand Old Man and was disgusted when, after his death,
the Parnellite Dublin Corporation threw out a proposal to
provide a site for a memorial statue.

Duffy's mind found respite from the ugliness of the
Parnell split in the consideration of Ireland's educational
and cultural needs. This, in effect, was what had brought
him into public life; and now in the early 1890's he began
to formulate again the thesis of the forties, the thesis of
Young Ireland, his own thesis, " educate that you may be
free ". In 1891, he was introducing the poems of John
O'Leary's sister, Ellen, and in the following year the theme
of his inauguaral lecture to the Irish Literary Society in
London of which he became the first President, was what
Irishmen might do for Irish literature. The Irish Literary
Society brought together many old friends estranged by the
disastrous political split and Duffy was one of the ' lions ' of
the season of 1892, as, active and able as ever, he went
everywhere and saw everybody. The distinguished biblio-
phile, J. S. Crone, was at a garden party given by Henry
Holiday, the artist, at his Hampstead home, and " gazed
with absorbed admiration at one who seemed to have
returned from another century, another world than ours ".
And as he grasped Duffy's hand, he thought how that hand
had once held those of Davis, Mangan, O'Connell, Mitchel,

Carleton, Smith O'Brien, Carlyle and Thackeray as well as those of several of the survivors of '98. And his heart warmed to hear Duffy's northern accent as fresh and strong as ever it was as he urged with an enthusiasm remarkable in a man of his years a publication venture that materialised shortly afterwards. It was a remarkable gathering of statesmen and soldiers, authors and artists, and among the ladies was the " queenly Maud Gonne ". F. Carruthers Gould was there and did a thumbnail sketch of Duffy smilingly reclining on a wicker chair.

In 1893, the year of the foundation of the Gaelic League, he spoke to the Society about books for the Irish people. No organised attempt was being made to raise the mind of the country to higher and more generous ideals of life and duty; the youthful mind which used to be kindled and purified by the poetry and legends of Ireland ran serious risks of becoming debased by battening on literary garbage. Liberty would do much for a people, but it would do little for them if they did not know or reverence their own ancestors. In any event the Irish people needed to be educated more intensively as well as nationally. He had seen multitudes of their bright intelligent young men arriving in Australia without profession, trade or training, and sinking to become waiters, barbers and cabmen. He argued for a revival of a love of noble books among the Irish people, saying that England held the sympathies of the communities which shared her blood, less by their obeying the same laws than by their loving the same books. But when he spoke of specific books he was thinking all the time of books of Irish interest in English.

His attitude to the Irish language was that of the Young Irelanders generally. In the first year *The Nation* printed at least two articles on the Irish language. They were by Davis, who, with John Pigot, earnestly wished for a wider extension of the use of Irish. Davis had learned some Irish

himself and was open to pressure from enthusiasts like
Nicholas Kearney, the secretary of the Drogheda Hibernian-
Celtic Society, and the scholar, John O'Donovan. Duffy was
constrained by Davis to use the Irish form of place-names
supplied by O'Donovan in the text of *The Nation's* ballads,
and he protested to MacNevin that they were going too far.
" It would need the authority of an Irish Parliament," he
wrote, " to get the present generation to spell Glengariff
Gleann Garbh." MacNevin agreed. Their task was not to
do with the nationality of Ollamh Fodhla and other gentlemen before and immediately after the Flood; but to elevate
the character of the people, raising up their bump of self-
esteem and suppressing the bump of servility. " We must be
cosmopolitan," he added, " and deviate occasionally from
our native bogs." Irish to MacNevin was thus a mere bog
language and a badge of serfdom while Ireland's survival lay
through the employment of English. In so thinking
MacNevin was at one with public men from well back in
the 18th century—Swift, for instance, thought that public
money would be well spent on eliminating such a nuisance—
and with O'Connell whose practical mind regarded the in-
cipient language movement as absurd. A diversity of lan-
guages, he used to say, was first imposed on mankind as a
curse at the building of Babel, and the superiority of English
as a medium of all modern communication was so great that
he saw without regret the gradual disuse of Irish. O'Connell,
therefore, contributed to the replacement of Irish by English
as the ordinary language of the Irish people but it is question-
able whether he did more harm in that respect than *The
Nation* and the English language ballads it so widely popu-
larised. During the period of the Australian " exile " Smith
O'Brien and Kevin Izod O'Doherty tried to learn Irish, but
R. D. Williams may have been expressing a more common
view in saying that all his patriotism could not persuade him
to follow suit. He could see no point in poring over a dead

language. He looked to the future and " the limitless domain
of ever-enlarging Science " rather than to the past.

Duffy personally behaved as if Irish did not exist and certainly felt no obligation to ensure its survival. His daughter,
Louise, one day came across a reference in a list of second-
hand books to O'Growney's *Simple Lessons in Irish*. It was
the first time she had heard of an Irish language. Her father
confirmed, when she went to him, that there was such a
thing; his mother had known it but did not teach it to him.
The only word of Irish he knew was " gearran " which meant
a horse. Davis, he told her, was the only one of his time
who was interested in Irish and his colleagues used to tease
him about it. A song that was then popular contained the
lines—

> Oh, let us go down
> To lovely Kingstown.

" Of course," they would say, " young Davis would want it
in Irish," and they suggested—

> Come down, my dearie,
> To pretty Dún Laoghaire.

Yet Duffy, like Mangan for instance, had acquired some
understanding of the quality of the old language from the
translations of folk material without feeling obliged to do
anything to preserve the language itself. He apparently
believed that it was possible to transfer the peculiar spirit of
the Irish originals into the English tongue so that Irish
nationality could prosper in the new medium. This was
doubtless what was in his mind when, in association with
Douglas Hyde and T. W. Rolleston, he found a London
publisher who was prepared to accept a series of books on
the lines of his old *Library of Ireland*, the first popular
printing enterprise in Ireland which came to an untimely end,
when only about half completed, through the Famine and
the collapse of the Young Ireland movement. Publication
in Ireland was originally intended and a company all but

established with representation on its board for contemporary
Irish writers when, according to W. B. Yeats, Duffy produced a letter from Archbishop Walsh warning him that
after his death the company would fall under a dangerous
influence and threw the project up. In this *New Irish
Library* series were printed Hyde's *History of Gaelic
Literature*, as well as Standish O'Grady's *Bog of Stars* and
Davis's hitherto unpublished *Patriot Parliament* which Duffy
personally resurrected. Indeed the revival of interest in
Davis, for which Duffy almost alone was responsible, gave
the Gaelic League and all the movements that sprang from
it the first political figure, who, in Daniel Corkery's phrase,
had intimations of the impossibility of a nationality continuing to survive when deprived of its language.

Duffy clashed acrimoniously with the young impatient
Yeats over the contents of the series. Yeats did not want
books for scholars so much as works of popular imaginative
literature. In his opinion, Young Ireland had deliberately
subordinated arts and letters to political ends and Duffy was
perpetuating the blunder. He assailed the patriotic verse of
the Young Irelanders, in particular Duffy's *Spirit of The
Nation*. The dispute had a political complexion, too, for
Yeats ranged the Parnellites and Fenians on his side against
the Irish Literary Society which included Unionists and anti-
Parnellites among its members; and one night, to the poet's
chagrin, some of them, at a meeting of the Society, assailed
the aged white-haired Duffy with shouts of " Remember
Newry " and " Here's to Mitchel that is gone, boys, gone."
Yeats, in describing this period, gives Duffy a taste of what
Duffy had given O'Connell and Mitchel. Duffy had arrived
from Australia, he said, bringing with him, among much
literary material, an unpublished novel into the middle of
which he had dropped a hot coal, so that nothing remained
but the borders of every page. His prose was undistinguished
in notable contrast to Mitchel "who had music and person-

ality, though rancorous and devil-possessed ". Nevertheless, Duffy had his way, but Davis's *Patriot Parliament* when published, though interesting in some aspects, and still of some historical value, had a dampening effect on the further commercial prospect of the series. Duffy never lost confidence, however, in the power of the printed word, and one of his last acts was to sell many of his rare books for the promotion of Irish literature and its circulation among the Irish people.

For his *New Irish Library* which ran to a dozen volumes in all, Martin MacDermott edited an anthology of ballads and songs written and published by the writers of *The Nation* since the death of Davis in 1845 which he called *The New Spirit of the Nation*. This was in effect a supplement to Duffy's *Spirit of the Nation* but it had not anything like the same vogue; it differed from it also in another respect, in that the editor found room in the collection for four of Duffy's own compositions. But, strangely enough, "The Muster of the North" was not one of them although the editor recalled that Richard Lalor Shiel had considered this equal to any piece of ballad poetry he had ever read, and that Duffy had been embarrassed when *The Times* praised it extravagantly, as he thought. MacDermott's own belief was that while Duffy had written many great and vigorous poems, poetry was not his greatest gift. " It was not poetry he brought to the party," he said, " so much as the power of initiation and organisation, without which, notwithstanding Davis's splendid talents, there would never have been a *Nation* newspaper, or a Young Ireland Party—any more than there would have been the old *Library of Ireland*, or the new. Davis did splendid work in the *Citizen*, and it fell dead ; splendid work in *The Register* in concert with John Dillon, and the circulation fell off. His first success was in *The Nation*, and it was attributable not only to his splendid

gifts but to the method with which that journal was organised, launched and sustained "—by Duffy, of course.

Yeats and MacDermott were nearer the truth than D'Arcy
McGee in their estimate of Duffy's work as a poet, but there
were others who shared McGee's opinion. T. W. Rolleston
said that none of the Young Irelanders wrote in rhyme and
metre with more sinewy force than Duffy. " His lines smite
home, like the axe of an Irish gallowglass; and though his
mind, as his whole career shows, was eminently that of a
statesman, he clearly thought and felt as a reckless fighter
when he faced the enemies of his cause with the keen blade
of verse in his hand." And Richard Dowling, in 1889, telling
Duffy that thirty years earlier when he had been working
on *The Nation* he had known most of his poems by heart,
recalled a sunny month in Tramore when all the hours of an
enchanted solitude were filled with Duffy's verses.

20

In July, 1894, when he was close on seventy-nine years of age, Duffy came to dinner in the House of Commons and members who entertained him found him brisk and bright after an operation for cataract. But a few years later he appeared to be going down the hill and abandoned the annual visit to Ireland whose green countryside used refresh his eyes after the parched mountains of the Riviera. He was practically blind and had to rely on his daughters and on Father John Fitzpatrick, an Oblate friend, to read to him and to write his letters. The reading lasted four or five hours a day because, apart from the newspapers, he loved stories— in particular, those of Scott, Thackeray and Conan Doyle. Essays and poetry he enjoyed, too. Edgar Allan Poe was a favourite of his, and he loathed the lofty newspaper gentle- men who patronised Poe as an eccentric creature, whom they felt entitled to pity and despise. " Poor Mangan," he told Richard Dowling, " was of the same rare school and was quite as caviare to the multitude. You will do better than these when you give yourself fair play by refusing to be sprightly, or smart, or sarcastic, or anything but natural." This reading chore was rather hard on the daughters; but it probably never occurred to Duffy that he was being inconsiderate; in those days it was not " the done thing " for young women to go out to work; so that some useful employment had to be found for them at home. After all, girls were only girls.

Duffy was concerned about the education of children and thought up schemes for providing them with penny readers, but he belonged to the old school of fathers who did not

associate with their offspring and was unable to communi-
cate with his own when they were very young and needed
him most. Louise says that they were all so much in awe
of their father that they could not speak naturally to him,
and the best he could do was to invite them to ask him
questions. "You know," he said, "I won't always be here."
He showed his temper, too, at times. Louise remembers him
berating a jarvey for driving too slowly; and for mispro-
nouncing the word "viscount" he told her that for an
intelligent girl she was as stupid as anyone could be.

When the children were grown up it was different; he
would then talk to them, for he loved nothing better than
company and conversation. So he was happy when the boys
of his first and second marriages came from Australia to
see him at Nice, and he could always unburden himself
somewhat to Susan and Harriet who were forty and twenty-
nine years of age respectively when their father's third wife,
younger than both of them, died following the birth of her
fourth child. Susan was a brilliant but shy and retiring
person who rarely spoke except in the family circle. But
in it she gave full expression to her sociable and happy
nature; she then drew on her entrancing memories of early
days in Australia of which the younger children never tired.
She had a distinct flair for writing also, and did in fact,
supply the Australian papers with articles from Nice,
some of which were later published in book form. In Melbourne while her own mother was busy bearing and rearing
children, she kept house and prepared meals for her father's
guests. His third marriage must have upset her and her
sisters, yet they never complained and when the necessity
arose they left Australia where they were very happy, to come
to a strange land, to serve their father, the great man to
whom they were so devoted and whom they would never
dream of criticising. Susan managed the house for him once
more and acted as his secretary, Harriet became his "doctor"

for increasingly he needed medical and nursing attention; the younger Geraldine alone was able to disport herself among her new French acquaintances, while all three devoted much affection and training to the young brothers and sister. Harriet and Geraldine worked in military hospitals during the 1914-18 War and received decorations and thanks from the French Government for their services.

For as long as he was able Duffy went for a walk every morning, often with Louise, and returned to enjoy the mid-day meal at which he could relax and reminisce. His talk sometimes turned on the old days and when it did it was to confirm the impression his books leave on the reader— that he was a hero-worshipper, a worshipper of Davis, of course, and of Dillon, but also of Carleton, and the Carlyles and especially Mrs. Carlyle. He had an abiding affection for Thomas O'Hagan which showed itself when he was sent to the Mairie to register the last of his many children. Manlike, he forgot the name his wife had chosen, but, without a moment's hesitation, he said, " We'll call him Thomas ", the Christian name of the two men he had loved most. Davis and O'Hagan.

Nice was always a popular place for holidays and many famous Irish people including John Dillon, the son of his old colleague, Douglas Hyde and the poetess, Dora Sigerson, visited Duffy there. Hyde, in his reminiscences, tells how he and his wife on their honeymoon in 1893 spent a whole day with him. "He was a first-rate raconteur and he told me how keen he was on stories in his youth and how he used to plague his mother to tell him another one, until finally she would say: ' Oh dear, I have no other story for you unless I told it to you in Irish.' That was enough ; it never occurred to him, even perhaps until that day I was with him, that he should have told her to speak Irish to him and to tell him stories in Irish. He did not understand that his mother was doing him an injustice. He said to me later, ' If anybody told me then (when he was in Ireland) that any four people would come together in a room to practise Irish, I would not believe him!'" Louise remembers Doctor Hyde's visit and how he—an excellent story-teller in his own right—kept the children breathless for hours over the exploits of the King of Ireland's son.

Duffy had local visitors, too, among them a French priest with whom he chatted in his indifferent French, and to whom he sometimes made his confession ; and the young British Vice-Consul, Joseph Wiseman Keogh, a Dublin man, whom he tried to teach to be proud that he was of the family of John Keogh, the leader of the Catholic cause in Ireland at the end of the eighteenth century. Duffy was, in fact, a popular figure until his pro-Boer attitude horrified the English colony.

He was a man of deep faith, a solid rather than a pious Catholic. He attended Mass every Sunday in a little Convent Chapel next door to his home in Nice and three or four times a year he went to Confession and Holy Communion, as was customary in his generation. With John O'Hagan he had a private pact to read the *Imitation of Christ* right through every year and to record the date when they had done so, and all his actions, public and private, were consistent with a fundamental sense of religion. When, for instance, a son of Lord O'Hagan died in the Boer war his immediate question was whether he had had the priest. He confessed in his *Ars Vitae* that he had never known except in glimpses and snatches the fervour of religious enthusiasm or the unspeakable tranquillity of religious rest, but à Kempis pointed out the way of peace to him. He copied into the scrapbook passages from the *Imitation* which enjoined the seeking of the will of God and the profit of one's neighbours as the means of enjoying internal liberty.

A plan of life that he sketched out for himself in 1864 and which he found " a great tranquillizer" showed his preoccupation with the after-life. "*The eternal future* which may begin for you soon," he wrote in a letter addressed to himself, " and is certainly not a great many years away, should become the subject of *habitual preparation*. There is a journey you must go; there is your residence for ever after! How small and poor are all our interests and ambitions compared with the duty of being ready for that journey . . . May God graciously please to awaken in your heart these feelings and resolutions . . . that you may be ready for the summons *more sure than day or night*".

In view of this it caused great pain to Duffy's family after his death when David Alec Wilson, the author of the *Life of Carlyle*, alleged that even before 1849 Duffy had outgrown Christianity and had only kept up a pretence of religion so as not to disturb his children. His daughter Susan's first letter of protest caused Wilson to admit that he had gone too far, that he should really have said that Duffy had outgrown orthodoxy. Later he promised to publish in his next edition a refutation of what he had written, but this never appeared as Wilson died before it could appear. The present writer has seen the correspondence and is inclined to share Susan's opinion of Wilson's unreliability and his capacity for attributing his own sentiments to other people.

Although the family must have expected that their father had not long to live, his death came quite unexpectedly on the 9th of February, 1903. There was nothing but a fainting fit to warn them. The priest came, Duffy made his confession and was anointed, and quietly passed away four hours later. There were no goodbyes; but Susan, Hetty and Geraldine who were at the bedside heard the dying man naming, house by house, the neighbours of his childhood in Monaghan town, and whispering a verse of John O'Hagan's; a bad poem, Yeats said it was, but its sentiments were sound and typified Duffy's ineradicable love of his country:

When comes the day all hearts to weigh
    If staunch they be or vile,
Shall we forget the sacred debt
    We owe our mother isle?
My native heath is brown beneath,
    My native waters blue ;
But crimson red o'er both shall spread,
    Ere I am false to you,
        Dear land !
    Ere I am false to you.

Duffy, who was survived by seven sons and four daughters, was buried at Nice but his ambition was to lay his bones in Ireland and to be kindly remembered there. So, it was appropriate when, at the request of the Lord Mayor of Dublin on behalf of a representative committee, which included Cardinal Logue and half the Irish hierarchy, he was subsequently brought home to be honoured publicly. His remains first lay before the altar in the Pro-Cathedral and there Archbishop Walsh made amends for Cardinal Cullen by chanting the requiem office with his priests and offering Mass for the soul of the last Young Irelander. On the eighth of March which was a Sunday, his coffin was followed to Glasnevin cemetery by a great concourse of people from all over Ireland and laid in a grave within the O'Connell circle near to that of John Blake Dillon. He had outlived his generation but he had made it live, too, for ever in his writings, and in the example of a life dedicated to the service of the people of Ireland and Australia. The very range of his activities in two continents singles him out from many of his contemporaries, while his achievements as the father of *The Nation*, as an educationist and particularly his policy of Independent Opposition made him at least the equal of Thomas Davis whose genius, demonstrated over a much shorter period, has hitherto caused him to be regarded as the outstanding figure in the Young Ireland movement. However, it is certain, from all we know of Duffy, that such comparisons would be odious to him, so perhaps we should leave Duffy and Davis and Dillon where they began, as the founding triumvirate of a movement whose ideological repercussions extend to our own days.

Sources

I. *Manuscript Material*

    Gavan Duffy Papers (National Library of Ireland).
    Gavan Duffy Papers (Royal Irish Academy).
    Ars Vitae (In author's possession).
    Chronicle of the Hughes Family written by Margaret Hughes
    (Mrs. Callan). (In the possession of the Callan family,
    Australia and New Zealand).

II. *Printed Material*

(a) Duffy's principal works: —

    Young Ireland: a fragment of Irish History, 1840-1845 (1880).
    Young Ireland, Part II or Four Years of Irish History, 1845-
    1849 (1883).
    The League of the North and South (1886).
    Thomas Davis: the Memoirs of an Irish Patriot 1840-1846
    (1890).
    Conversations with Carlyle (1892).
    My Life in Two Hemispheres (2 vols.) (1898).

(b) Other works consulted: —

    Black, R. D. Collison, *Economic Thought and the Irish Question,
    1817-1870* (Cambridge, 1960).

    Clarke, Randall, *The Relations between O'Connell and the
    Young Irelanders* (Irish Historical Studies, March 1942).

    Corish, Patrick, *Cardinal Cullen and The National Association of
    Ireland* (in Reportorium Novum, vol. 3, No. 1, Dublin,
    1961-62).

    Curtis, L. P. Jr., *Coercion and Conciliation in Ireland, 1880-1892*
    (Princeton, 1963).

    Daunt, W. J. O'N., *Eighty-five years of Irish History* (London,
    1886).

    De hIde, Dubhghlas, *Mise agus an Connradh* (Dublin, 1937).

    De Vere White, Terence, *The Road to Excess* (Dublin, 1945).

    Edwards, R. Dudley, *The contribution of Young Ireland to
    the development of the national idea* (Féilscríbhinn Tórna,
    Cork, 1947).

    —(ed. with T. Desmond Williams) *The Great Famine* (Dublin,
    1956).

Guiney, Louise Imogen, *James Clarence Mangan* (Norwood, Mass., U.S.A., 1897).

Gwynn, Denis, *Daniel O'Connell* (Cork, 1947).

— *O'Connell, Davis and the Colleges Bill* (Cork, 1948).

— *Young Ireland and 1848* (Cork, 1949).

Hammond, J. L., *Gladstone and the Irish Nation* (London, 1938).

Hone, Joseph, *W. B. Yeats 1865-1939* (London, 1943).

Inglis, Brian, *The Freedom of the Press in Ireland, 1784-1841* (London, 1944).

Kiernan, T. J., *The Irish Exiles in Australia* (Dublin, 1954).

Lucas, E., *The Life of Frederick Lucas, M.P.* (2 vols.) (London, 1886).

McCartney, Donal, *Lecky's Leaders of Public Opinion in Ireland* (Irish Historical Studies, Sept. 1964).

ed. McDermott, Martin, *The New Spirit of the Nation* (London 1894).

McDowell, R. B., *Public Opinion and Government Policy 1801-1846* (London, 1952).

McGee, T. D'Arcy, *Memoir of Charles Gavan Duffy* (Dublin, 1849).

McGrath, Fergal, *Newman's University: Idea and Reality* (London, 1951).

McIntyre, Angus, *The Liberator* (London, 1965).

ed. MacManus, M. J., *Thomas Davis and Young Ireland* (Dublin, 1945).

MacNamara, Brinsley, *Charles Gavan Duffy* (in *Thomas Davis and Young Ireland*) (Dublin, 1945).

MacSuibhne, Peadar, *Paul Cullen and his contemporaries* (3 vols.) (Naas, 1961-1965).

Mitchel, John, *Jail Journal* (New York, 1854).

Moody, T. W., *Thomas Davis 1814-45* (Dublin, 1945).

Moore, M. G., *An Irish Gentleman—George Henry Moore* (London, 1913).

Norman, E. R., *The Catholic Church and Ireland in the Age of Rebellion* (London, 1965).

— *The Catholic Church and Irish Politics in the Eighteen Sixties* (Dublin Historical Association, 1965).

Nowlan, Kevin B., *Charles Gavan Duffy and the Repeal Movement* (National University of Ireland, 1963).

— *The Politics of Repeal* (London, 1965).

O'Brien, R. Barry, *The Life of Parnell* (London, 1899).

— *Irish Memories* (London, 1904).

O'Brien, William (with Desmond Ryan), *Devoy's Post Bag* (2 vols.) (Dublin, 1948).

Ó Cuiv, Brian, *Irish Dialects and Irish-speaking Districts* (Dublin, 1951).

O'Hegarty, P. S., *A History of Ireland under the Union, 1801-1922* (London, 1952).

O'Leary, John, *Recollections of Fenians and Fenianism* (London, 1896).

Ó Néill, Tomás, *Fiontán Ó Leathlobhair* (Dublin, 1962).

O'Sullivan, T. F., *The Young Irelanders* (Tralee, 1944).

Serle, Geoffrey, *The Golden Age, a history of the Colony of Victoria, 1851-1961* (Melbourne, 1963).

Sheridan, John D., *James Clarence Mangan* (Dublin, 1937).

Sullivan, A. M., *New Ireland* (London, 1877).

Sullivan, T. D., *Recollections of Troubled Times in Irish Politics* (Dublin, 1905).

Thornley, David, *Isaac Butt and Home Rule* (London, 1964).

ed. Tierney, Michael, *Daniel O'Connell* (Dublin, 1949).

Trevelyan, George Otto, *Life and Letters of Lord Macaulay* (2 vols.) (London, 1876).

Tynan, Katherine, *Memories* (London, 1924).

Whyte, J. H., *The Independent Irish Party 1850-9* (Oxford, 1958).

— *Fresh Light on Archbishop Cullen and the Tenant League* (Irish Ecclesiastical Record, March 1953).

— *The Tenant League and Irish Politics in the eighteen-fifties* (Dublin, 1963).

ed. Williams, T. Desmond (see R. Dudley Edwards).

Wilson, David Alec, *Thomas Carlyle* (5 vols.) (London, 1923-9).

Woodham-Smith, Cecil, *The Great Hunger 1845-9* (London, 1962).

Yeats, W. B., *Autobiographies* (London, 1926).

INDEX